HEALTHY JAPANESE COOKING

SIMPLE RECIPES FOR A LONG LIFE, THE SHOKU-IKU WAY

BY MAKIKO SANO

Photography by Lisa Linder

QUADRILLE

CONSCIOUS EATING

p.6		The power of five
p.16		Foundation dishes

p.24	煮る	Simmer
p.44	蒸す	Steam and microwave
p.66	焼く	Broil, grill, and fry
p.86	混ぜる	No-cook
p.100	寿司	Five senses sushi

Japanese Pickles, see page 90

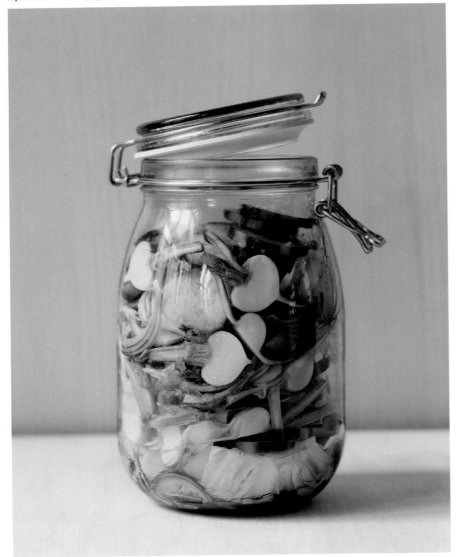

CONSCIOUS EATING

Healthy Japanese Eating is about having a brand new relationship with food. It is conscious eating: ditching that just-grab-something attitude and believing that you deserve to be a little more mindful about the relationship between what you eat and your body. It is about choosing foods based on their power to invigorate, enliven, energize, fuel, and give you true nutrition. When you do this you simply feel better, lighter, and in control and—though initially you will have to put some thought into it—over time it will become a way of life.

My family instilled this mindful attitude to food in me as a child in Japan. Every morning my grandfather had a pint of water mixed with the juice of two squeezed lemons. I had to drink it with him (and I thought it was disgusting as a child!), but I still do the same to this day. We ate a selection of fish, vegetables, beans, and miso soup at every meal. My grandfather played tennis until he was 97; my uncle lived to 100. Growing up, my memories are of my parents, aunts and uncles, grandparents, and cousins, all of whom lived nearby, eating their evening meal together.

Sagen Ishizuka initiated the Shoku-Iku concept. This famous Japanese military doctor was also a pioneer of the macrobiotic diet. The philosophy is built on acquiring knowledge about what we eat, how we prepare it, and how we put different foods together. The rules of Shoku-Iku are not strict or hard to follow, but truly common sense.

A Shoku-Iku way of eating is to create a few dishes—not just one alone—to place on the table and share. Even at breakfast, my mother will always have a wide selection of foods: an oil-free omelet, spinach or nori salad, miso soup, and a piece of fruit. I love the idea of sharing food, as it makes each meal an occasion. It's great that even when I was a teenager, busy with friends and school, we still made time to sit as a family. And if you live alone, take the time to make a couple of quick and simple side dishes, to celebrate each mealtime, honor your body, and become more of a conscious eater.

This attention to the ritual of mealtimes will also help you to incorporate more variety in your diet; what we call the power of five. As you will read over the next few pages, this philosophy is to eat foods from five food groups that appeal to your five senses, that contain five tastes, and which aim to reflect five colors.

The recipes in this book are mostly gluten-free, but those that are not can easily be tweaked to suit a gluten-free diet. They are often, as is the Japanese way, rice based and rice is very easily digested. Many of the recipes swap meat for what we know in Japan as "the meat of the garden," in other words vegetable protein sources such as beans and pulses. The recipes are largely dairy-free, as Japanese cuisine rarely features dairy produce.

All the recipes in this book use the healthiest cooking methods possible. Certainly there is no need to turn your oven on (or even to own an oven), and in some cases, no cooking is required at all. The dishes are revitalizing and tasty, but also simple, quick to prepare, and budget friendly. Many of the dishes—and all the sauces—can be made in quantity and stored for later, to help cut down on food waste... Welcome to Healthy Japanese Eating!

GO SHOKU-IKU!

Eat as wide a variety of foods as you can every day.

Choose locally grown and seasonal foods.

Establish a healthy rhythm to your daily meals, eating at regular times.

Choose to sit down, consciously enjoy, and focus on your meals.

If you have a family, treat mealtime as something sacred that you all do together.

Think about what you have eaten through the day and make the next meal choice something different, to balance your food groups.

Don't skip meals. It will lead to poor food choices later in the day.

Combine vegetables, fruits, milk, fish, and beans in your daily diet. Avoid too much salt, sugar, or fat.

The power of five

Colors
Tastes
Senses
Food groups
Cooking methods

The five colors

Learning to adopt the principles of the power of five into your daily diet is the key to unlocking a whole new way of eating. This Buddhist tradition arrived in Japan in the sixth century and is part of our way of life. By combining elements of all these colors in your meals whenever possible, you broaden the variety of foods you eat and ensure you are getting the healthiest mix of essential vitamins and minerals. My grandmother used to aim to eat 30 different foods a day. That is hard... but you should aim for 13 to 20 different foods every day. In other words, look at your eating habits and see if you focus on the same food types and colors—such as pasta—too heavily.

A food rainbow
We have become adept at checking prepacked sandwiches for their calorie count, but we perhaps still don't think too carefully about the breadth of the food groups we choose from daily. In Japanese cooking we get automatic variety, because of the ever-present side dishes. A Japanese bento box, for instance, might include white rice with black sesame seeds, a red umeboshi (salt plum), a slice of sweet yellow omelet, and green beans with black sesame sauce.

Look to see where you can incorporate this idea into your food choices. For example, if you pick up a sandwich at lunchtime, pick up a pot of edamame beans as well. Choose a sunshine-colored fruit juice to accompany it. If you fancy a piece of lean steak, prepare a freshly chopped tomato salad on the side. You don't have to ditch the things you love. Just make sure you have a mix every day of your life.

Pick and mix
In our supermarket shop we tend to buy the same things week in week out, and this goes against the quest for variety. When you look at your shopping basket, it should reflect the five colors. Here are some ingredients you might want to start adding to your shop and using to create my Shoku-Iku dishes.

Green/blue

Broccoli
the intensely blue-green vegetable contains 150% of your daily vitamin C needs in a 100g [1½ cup] serving.

Spinach
this deep garden-green vegetable is considered a superfood, as it is bursting with iron and potassium.

Edamame beans
a complete protein, with all nine essential amino acids. Also chock-full of vitamins B, C, and K, even when frozen and defrosted.

Cucumber
the green skin is full of vitamin C, but this hydrating vegetable also contains silicon and sulfur, associated with reducing the risk of some cancers.

Red/orange

Carrot
the color comes from high levels of antioxidant beta-carotene, which we convert into vitamin A.

Tomato
bursting with vitamins A, C, and E and also rich in flavonoids; natural anti-inflammatories.

Sweet potato
another glorious orange- or purple-fleshed vegetable, rich with beta-carotene. A dash of fat, such as olive oil, helps the body release beta-carotene's benefits. My mom would wrap sweet potatoes in foil and bake them in the fire as an after-school snack. Delicious.

White

Cabbage
a great source of fiber. Use it fresh to make the most of its anti-inflammatory goodness and its rich potassium content.

Daikon
not only is this root vegetable highly flavorsome, but it contains anti-carcinogenic phytochemicals and has decongestant properties.

Napa cabbage
these pale leaves are intensely hydrating, low in calories, and aid sleep.

Fish
a major source of omega-3 fatty acids, this can help to protect against a range of diseases, from cancer to heart disease, depression to arthritis.

White rice
a digestive aid and natural anti-inflammatory. Its protein is important for preserving lean body mass. Its manganese helps boost the immune system, while thiamine is important for cognitive processes.

Black/brown

Shiitake mushrooms
known for their immune system support, these are a good source of iron and antioxidants.

Buckwheat
this not only helps in keeping cholesterol levels low, but is also a good source of magnesium.

Seaweed
great for detoxing the system, this is rich in enzymes that aid digestion. It is also high in fiber.

Brown rice
rich in selenium, which reduces the risk of heart disease. It is also a slow energy release food, keeping you fuller for longer.

Black beans
the skins are an incredible source of phytonutrients. More fiber than chickpeas or lentils.

Black sesame seeds
rich in magnesium and calcium (found in the husk), the numerous health benefits of which include combatting disruptive sleep patterns. I crush the seeds in a mini-blender to ensure I keep all the goodness of the husk and store them in small jars.

Yellow

Soybeans
very rich in protein and manganese and a good source of iron, magnesium, and copper. High in the phytoestrogens beneficial for menopausal women.

Pumpkin
plenty of fiber to keep you feeling full and a great source of unsaturated fat. The high beta-carotene content is essential for glowing skin.

Corn
a sunshine vegetable, rich in B vitamins and fiber.

The five tastes

Surprising palates is one way to get people to connect with what they are eating. Awakening all five tastes has been part of my culinary journey; it is when you trigger them that food really comes alive.

Cooking with fresh, healthy ingredients need never be a bland option. It is how you compose those tastes, what other flavors you balance them with, that makes meals exciting. Many of my recipes can use different sauces, depending on which taste you crave at that moment.

Sweet

Sweet tastes signal the presence of carbohydrates. In Japan, we eat only very small amounts of sweet things. One slice of cake would be shared between four people. It was appreciated more that way... you learned to truly savor sweet things. My great uncle still had all his teeth at 97! Many traditional Japanese sweets have alternatives to refined sugar at their base, for instance red bean paste or fruit, letting the fructose do the work. One of my favorite sweet ingredients is mirin, a sweet rice wine essential in Japanese cooking. You can make your own mirin by gently heating three parts of sake or vodka with one part of sugar.

Sour

Sour = acidity. Japanese rice vinegar delivers that sour hit, but is slightly less acidic and sweeter than its European counterpart. It is this vinegar added to sushi rice that adds that satisfying note, bringing the rice alive. The juice and zest of citrus fruits are of course the other familiar providers of sour taste sensations. The Japanese yuzu citrus is just being discovered here. This cross between a lemon, grapefruit, and mandarin orange contains three times more vitamin C than a lemon, elevating it to a superfood in the sour realms.

Bitter

This is the most sensitive of all the tastes, not least because it helps us avoid foods that might not be good for us, or which may be under-ripe. However, it is a very complementary flavor when used sparingly, or with the right companions: think of how green olives flatter an aperitif. Some vegetables have a slightly bitter tone, such as eggplant, or spinach. Again, when cooked with complementary flavors, the bitterness adds a delicious roundness. My Lemon soy sauce dressing (see page 20) has delectable bitter notes.

Salt

As a chef, I am super-aware of the issues around salt. In Japan, the main source of salt in food is from soy sauce and miso. Unlike western chefs, though, and as you will see through the Shoku-Iku recipes, we tend to add very little salt during cooking. Nearly all the salt comes from the sauces or condiments used, so there is less "hidden salt" than there can be in western food.

Soy sauce does contain the high levels of sodium found in table salt, but the fermentation process also produces peptides, which may limit the cardiovascular issues related to regular salt. Either way, try to look for traditionally made soy sauce; those from Japan usually are. You can also purchase low-sodium varieties. Recent studies on miso intake among Japanese adults have also shown that miso-containing diets tend to lower the risk of cardiovascular problems, despite its salt content. Since miso is seldom eaten alone, other cardio-supportive foods in miso soups and stir-fries might also play an important role.

Umami

The name of this subtle, pleasant savory taste comes from the Japanese word "umai," meaning delicious. It is a naturally occurring flavor found in the oils of certain vegetables, meat, and fish. First recognized in Japan in 1908, the flavor was detected in asparagus, tomatoes, cheese, and meat. However, another Japanese staple was where the umami flavor shone brightest. Dashi is a rich, tasty stock made from kombu (kelp) and often bonito flakes (for vegetarian or fish-based recipes, see page 18). It is widely used as a base in Japanese cooking. The essence of its savory deliciousness is imparted by amino acids called glutamates. My Everyday soy sauce dressing (see page 19) has delicious umami flavors. You can also dial up the umami quotient of your food if you eat dairy, by adding a little butter to a soy sauce-based dish, or sprinkling a bit of Parmesan cheese into a miso sauce.

The five senses

How often have you sat down to eat without consciously thinking about the effects your food is having on you? Perhaps most of the time? All of the time? The underlying principle of Shoku-Iku asks us to be mindful and fully awake to all five senses: taste, smell, sight, sound, and touch. Too often we are in too much of a hurry. Taking time to eat slowly, so you can be more aware of your senses, is really important.

In Japan, fulfilling all the senses is second nature. It reconnects us to what we are eating.

Sound

I love to experience the sounds of different restaurants depending on the food they are creating. From the quiet stillness of a high-end ryotei restaurant, where due respect is shown for the exquisitely prepared sushi dishes, to the happy, boisterous noise of an izakaya (Japanese tapas bar). It's as if the food invokes a certain atmosphere. At home, if you are bringing a selection of dishes to the table for a sharing meal, it always creates a jovial, bonding, informal, and light-hearted atmosphere. But listening to the sounds of food is also key to our enjoyment. The crisp crunch of fresh vegetables is, in itself, invigorating and some researchers think sound can influence and enhance flavor. Top chef Heston Blumenthal famously gives his diners headphones to enhance specific dishes with their own soundtrack!

Sight

Seeing a plate of vibrant colors is uplifting and appetizing. In Japan, even a lunchtime bento box is filled with color: yellow omelet, bright green edamame, pink salmon, white rice, and black sesame seeds. Once you get used to seeing these kinds of colors, other foods can appear bland. You can easily dial up the vibrancy of whatever you are cooking simply by the addition of bright pickles, a scattering of shredded nori, or some sliced cherry tomatoes. Even consider your tableware. In Japan, food presentation has been raised to an art form, but just having a selection of beautiful dishes, bowls and utensils elevates what you have prepared and makes it that bit more enticing.

Touch

Touch is vital to me as a chef, whether it's learning how to handle food, or eating and appreciating its various textures. Even the very act of chopping herbs, sprinkling seeds, or rolling sushi connects me to what I am preparing and therefore to what I am about to eat. It also helps you to eat a good variety of foods; you wouldn't want everything to "feel" the same.

Carry that same sense into your tableware. Japanese meals often require you to pick up vessels of miso, dishes of pickles, or eat with chopsticks. Connecting with the smooth wood of a bamboo chopstick, the delicate touch of a porcelain dish, or the rougher texture of a stoneware bowl adds to the overall sensation experience.

Smell

Through my recipes you will learn to prepare food with some of the more underused cooking processes. Steaming is a method I love, not least because as you steam food, a host of delicious scents rise into the air. The sense of smell starts the longing to taste the food. Eighty percent of what we perceive to be the flavor of food is actually down to its aroma. Smell also opens up our memory pathways. There's something very comforting about preparing a food whose scent takes you back to a place in your childhood or a happy event.

Taste

Ultimately, taste elevates food from a simple question of nourishment to a pleasurable experience. As you become more familiar with Japanese dishes, you will see that many of the taste twists come from extra condiments, sauces, and sprinkles: the umami flavor of a splash of dashi; the deep saltiness of soy sauce; the heat of a little sake or wasabi. Minced nori, shiso leaves and citrusy yuzu zest shavings are other things you may learn to experiment with, to excite the taste buds and give your food an authentic Japanese feel, along with mirin, vinegar, and ginger.

Japanese Garden, see page 60

The five food groups

In East Asian tradition, the number five has always been important. The traditional Japanese calendar has a five day weekly cycle, while much of the Japanese aesthetic is built around the five elements of water, fire, earth, metal, and air: the flame under a nabemono cooking pot; the sound of a water feature in a courtyard.

The foundation of Shoku-Iku eating is based around this principle of five, in this case five food groups, which you should select from every day. When I'm eating out in Japan I am always struck by how groups of diners, even without thinking, balance out their food choices. It's as if they subconsciously know what is missing and will order an extra dish to balance out what they have already selected.

Grains
(aim for 5 to 6 servings a day)

Grains (including rice and noodles) are an important source of nutrients and dietary fiber. They are high in several B vitamins (thiamine, riboflavin, niacin, and folate) and minerals (iron, magnesium, and selenium). These play key roles in both our metabolism and boosting our nervous and immune systems. They also help the body release energy from protein, fats, and carbohydrates. Their fiber content may help to lower cholesterol and maintain a healthy heart. Because of their iron content they also help maintain iron levels in the blood, which is especially beneficial for women. To make the most of their nutrients, combine them with vitamin C-rich foods and eat them with proteins and carbohydrates.

Tip: When preparing white rice, always rinse it first under cold running water until the water runs clear (see page 110 for how to cook Japanese rice).

The five elements

As with a macrobiotic diet, Shoku-Iku is all about balance through variety, making sure you acknowledge all five elements (wood, fire, earth, water, metal) in your daily meals.

Once you get used to balancing from the food groups, you can adjust them according to your mood. To feel more grounded, make sure you take in enough earth foods; to help increase your stamina, up the fire foods. If you are feeling a little withdrawn, cut down on metal foods.

WOOD	FIRE	EARTH	METAL	WATER
Leafy green vegetables, raw, steamed or simmered, vinegars and lemon.	Garlic, ginger, scallions, mild spices, nuts, and seeds.	Sweet root and ground vegetables cooked into a soup or stew.	Pressure-cooked or long-cooked grains such as brown rice, daikon, and pickles.	Miso soups, bean soups, miso.

Vegetables

(aim for 5 to 6 servings a day)

When trying to balance your diet, keeping a food diary for a week can be a real eye opener. As with the usual nutritional advice, ensuring you eat adequate quantities of vegetables every day is vital. If you are choosing too many comfort foods, then starting to adjust this to fulfil your daily quota is made easier by preparing dishes already laden with vegetables.

High in dietary fiber and antioxidants, vegetables should be the cornerstone to every meal. If you're not cooking a vegetarian or vegetable-filled dish then add a side dish of green salad leaves or grated carrot, or nibble on an appetizer of radishes, red pepper sticks, or edamame. These strategies can easily up your vegetable intake with virtually no effort. My Japanese garden (see page 60) is made with pumpkin, turnip, daikon, broccoli, and snow peas, so there are five vegetables in one dish.

Fish and meat, eggs and beans, nuts and seeds

(aim for 3 to 5 servings a day)

Protein is a vital source of nutrients, for healthy bones, muscles, skin, and blood. With fats and carbohydrates, proteins also provide the calories we need.

In Japan, the majority of our protein comes from fish. Not only is fish high in omega-3 fatty acids, but it is inherently lean. When choosing meat, always select lean cuts of pork, chicken, or beef.

Tip: we often sprinkle fish with sake before cooking, to refresh the surface and remove "fishy" odors.

The alternative to fish and meat, highly popular in Japan, are soybeans. We refer to these as "the meat of the garden" and they have all the benefits of protein but with none of the downsides.

Eggs are another great and easy source of protein and feature in Japanese cooking often, especially at breakfast time when an omelet is a favorite.

Not just an afterthought, nuts and seeds should also be part of your daily food. These little extras are packed with nutrients including B vitamins, vitamin E, iron, zinc, and magnesium.

Tip: For a lighter option to a bowl of nuts, munch on some salted edamame beans (also packed with protein).

Fruits

(aim for 2 to 3 servings a day)

Other than the obvious vitamin and fiber benefits of fruit, one of the bonuses to a chef is that it contains natural sugars (fructose). Refined sugars are known dietary baddies and I try to steer clear. In many of my dessert recipes I use fruit to add sweetness, especially when the fruit has been poached or steamed, reducing its juices to a sweet sticky sauce.

The five food groups of Shoku-Iku encourage the cutting down to a bare minimum of sugary sweets. If you can limit your sweet intake and start to think of fruit as your sweet treat, you will improve your overall diet. A few slices of nashi (Japanese pear), melon, or ume (Japanese plum), made into balls and wrapped in rice make a delicious treat. And check out my Fruit buns recipe (see page 65).

Dairy

(no more than 2 servings a day)

In modern-day Japan, all manner of cheeses and dairy products can be found on the streets, thanks to the pizza and coffee companies that are springing up. However, dairy was not historically part of the diet and is still little used in home cooking. Japanese hot drinks of green tea or miso don't require the addition of milk. A Japanese breakfast seldom includes cereal and milk, although my mother does like to eat yogurt at breakfast time. There are certain indulgent treats we do love—green tea ice cream is a particular favorite—but for the most part, milk is not a common ingredient in a Japanese kitchen.

The five cooking methods

The cooking method is vital to the appearance, flavor and texture of a dish. Japanese cooks hardly ever roast food, but that's not to say we don't employ plenty of other methods. Take kaiseki cuisine, for instance, the Japanese chef's art of using various cooking styles to add up to a complete experience. Kaiseki meals usually start with the most delicate flavors and textures, such as a few slices of sashimi. This is followed by soup or simmered vegetables in broth. Next is grilled fish or meat. The meal then winds down with rice, soup, and pickles. Dessert is always light; perhaps a perfect slice of melon, or a refreshing dish of green tea ice cream. While none of us would produce that on a daily basis, it is easy to make three or four simple dishes, for example, grilled fish, miso soup, and steamed or raw vegetables, that echo the principle.

All the techniques I favor are gentle on the food— retaining the nutrients—and also quick.

Steam and microwave

Many of my recipes are cooked by steaming, which is a beautifully simple, gentle, and traditional way of cooking food. But as a busy mother, I also use the microwave as a super-speedy way of producing the same results. Heavenly steamed sea bream (see page 47) can be made in the microwave and is ready to eat in four minutes.

– **Steaming has a myriad of benefits. It not only retains food's nutrients, but also its moisture and freshness.**

– **Both steaming and microwaving help retain the vibrant colors and natural flavors of your food.**

– **Steaming softens food fibers, making them easily digestible.**

– **When you steam a meal, there is no need for cooking oil or fat, so your food is lighter and healthier. And, because you can stack steamer dishes over a single heat source, it saves time, energy, and money.**

Simmer

Simmering is an essential part of Japanese cooking. Nimono is a home-cooking style of simmering vegetables in seasoned broth. Shabu is its grander restaurant style, where a central bowl of simmered broth is used to "wash" or lightly cook julienned vegetables and meats (see page 41). The key to simmering is low heat. This avoids the drab, soggy effects of high heat boiling. In Japan, the liquid from a simmered dish becomes part of the sauce.

– **Many of my recipes simmer and steam in shallow lidded pans with only a tiny amount of liquid.**

– **Simmering preserves the vibrant colors of the food.**

– **Liquids other than water can be used to add more flavor.**

Broil, grill, and fry

I love the scents that waft from food as you broil or grill it. Many of the broiled or grilled Shoku-Iku recipes for fish, meat, and vegetables have been marinated or "rinsed" with flavoring ingredients, heightening that mouth-watering effect. The benefits over shallow frying or roasting are many.

– **Excess fats drip off and cook away, leaving less fat in the food.**

– **Vegetables retain more vitamins and minerals.**

– **The high heat seals in moisture and keeps food tender, so there's no need to add oil or butter.**

No-cook

Raw food is a way of life in Japan and not just in the well-known sushi and sashimi. The benefits of raw foods are tremendous.

– **Our bodies love the electrons that raw foods preserve and which are diminished in cooking: they literally burn up and break down.**

– **Cooking food destroys many of its natural enzymes. We need these enzymes to break down nutrients.**

- Essential vitamins and minerals are lost through the cooking process. Many nutritionists believe we should be eating one raw dish or accompaniment at every meal, for example, fruit with breakfast, salad with lunch, and sashimi at dinner.

- Raw fruit and veg tend to be more bulky with fiber, so help keep us feeling fuller for longer. They also have a high natural water content, so they hydrate as well as nourish.

- Chewing raw food is an excellent workout for your gums and jaw. The Japanese are crazy about chewing. We really see it as essential exercise and will deliberately select foods that require more chewing.

Sushi

This is the food most associated with Japanese cuisine across the world. In its traditional form, sushi delivers all the goodness of raw fish, which has always been Shoku-Iku and, these days, that researchers increasingly believe is one of the keys to a long and healthy life. I have also included some new ways with sushi in this book, including lightly cooked vegetables, for vegetarian and vegan diets.

- Ideal for entertaining, Shoku-Iku sushi dishes are stunning looking, appealing to the sense of sight, as well as taste.

- Rice is light on the digestion, so a sushi meal is easy for your body to process.

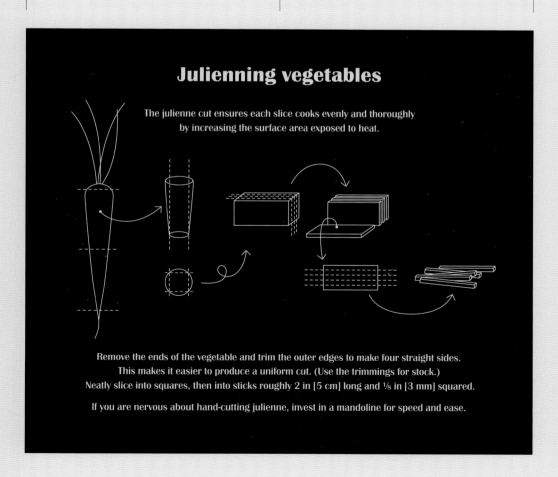

Julienning vegetables

The julienne cut ensures each slice cooks evenly and thoroughly by increasing the surface area exposed to heat.

Remove the ends of the vegetable and trim the outer edges to make four straight sides.
This makes it easier to produce a uniform cut. (Use the trimmings for stock.)
Neatly slice into squares, then into sticks roughly 2 in [5 cm] long and ⅛ in [3 mm] squared.

If you are nervous about hand-cutting julienne, invest in a mandoline for speed and ease.

Foundation dishes

All-rounder sauces and stocks

These are the foundations to all Shoku-Iku dishes. Once you have learned how to create these, you can mix and match, using them to add the flavors you like to most Shoku-Iku recipes.

Stocks

Basic dashi (stock)

Dashi is a fundamental building block of Japanese food. It is a stock, usually made from bonito flakes, dried kelp, and sometimes, dried sardines or anchovies. There are no animal fats in it at all.

My grandmother would mix them herself to make her meals. My basic stock these days is made from packaged dried kelp and bonito flakes. Feel free to scale the recipe down if you don't think you'll need this much. You can use it immediately, or cover and keep it in the fridge for five to seven days (or up to one month in the freezer).

Makes 8 cups/2 qt [2 L]
— 10 x 2-in [5-cm] pieces of dried kelp
— 5 cups [50 g] bonito flakes

Pour 8 cups/2 qt [2 L] water into a saucepan. Add the kelp and set aside for at least 1 hour and up to 3 or 4 if you have time. The deeply savory, umami flavor of the kelp will seep into the water.

Set the saucepan over medium heat and bring it to a boil. Reduce the heat to its lowest when the kelp starts "dancing" (as my grandmother used to say.) Cook at the gentlest simmer for 20 to 30 minutes. Turn off the heat and add ½ cup of water to cool it down.

Add the bonito flakes and leave for about one minute. Strain the stock through a sieve into a bowl, pressing down on the bonito flakes with a spoon to extract the maximum flavor.

Vegetarian dashi

Makes about 4 cups/1 qt [1 L]
— 5⅝-in [1.5-cm] pieces of dried kelp
— 5 dried shiitake mushrooms

Pour 4 cups/1 qt [1 L] cold water into a glass bowl or pot. Add the kelp and shiitake mushrooms. Cover and refrigerate for at least 6 hours (I usually leave it overnight). Strain through a sieve into a bowl, pressing down with a spoon for the maximum flavor.

Motoko's (my mother's) dashi

A dashi made with this as its liquid base has more flavor than the others and is more nutritious, due to the goodness of brown rice. It is meant to form the liquid part of the two dashis to the left.

— ¼ cup [50 g] brown rice

Rinse the rice and put it into a medium saucepan. Set over medium heat and cook, stirring, until the husks start to split. You will know when this happens; you can see it (but you may need a bit of practice to spot it), so go by your nose: you will smell the brown rice aroma when the husk splits to release its flavor.

Pour in 4 cups/1 qt [1 L] water and cook on medium-low heat (enough so the rice is "dancing") for 30 minutes.

Pass through a sieve into a bowl and top up with liquid to form the base of a Basic or Vegetarian dashi.

Noodle soup stock

This is easy, made from very basic Japanese ingredients and, of course, my dashi stock.

Makes about 5 cups [1.2 L]
— 3¼ cups [800 ml] Basic or Vegetarian dashi (see left)
— ⅞ cup [200 ml] mirin
— ⅞ cup [200 ml] soy sauce

Add everything to a saucepan and bring to a simmer.

Soup stock

This one is, if anything, even easier, as you don't even need a pre-prepared dashi stock.

Makes about 5 cups [1.2 L]
— ⅞ cup [200 ml] mirin
— ⅞ cup [200 ml] soy sauce
— 1 cup [10 g] bonito flakes
— 2 in [5 cm] piece of dried kelp

Pour the mirin into a saucepan and bring to a boil. Add the soy sauce, pour in 3¼ cups [800 ml] water and return to a boil. Add the bonito flakes and kelp and turn off the heat. Let it cool. Keep in the fridge and use within 10 days.

Dressings

In Japanese food, we use a lot of dressings, together with small amounts of sauce, to add flavor to our dishes. This is because traditional Japanese food is quite plain, especially in a Shoku-Iku style of eating, without many strong tastes. So it's nice to add additional flavors into the food. Many contain soy sauce and we enjoy its umami flavor.

These dressings are not thick; they are light and tasty, not high in calories or oily, and you can use them for anything you like—salad, chicken, or fish, or even with sushi. So, next time you reach for the mayonnaise, remember these lighter recipes and give them a try instead.

Everyday soy sauce dressing

The name says it all: there's almost no Japanese dish that this won't complement.

Makes enough for 4
— 2 Tbsp mirin
— 2 Tbsp soy sauce, ideally light soy sauce
— 2 Tbsp rice vinegar

Pour all the ingredients into a saucepan and heat to a simmer, then allow the pan to cool completely. Covered and kept in the fridge, the dressing will last for 7 days.

Sweet soy dressing

This is nice with meat, shrimp, or salads.

Makes enough for 4
— 2 tsp runny honey
— 4 tsp whole grain mustard
— 4 tsp lemon juice
— 3 Tbsp grapeseed oil
— Pinch of salt

Mix all the ingredients together well.

Sesame salad sprinkle dressing

If you eat whole sesame seeds, they go straight through you. But, if you blend them to a powder, you get all their nutrition. Whenever one of my recipes calls for "crushed" sesame seeds, it means seeds whizzed to a powder in a blender.

This is especially good with quite plain steamed dishes, or over salads.

Makes enough for 4
— 1 Tbsp soy sauce
— 2 Tbsp superfine sugar
— 3 Tbsp rice vinegar
— 1 Tbsp white miso
— 2 Tbsp white sesame seeds, crushed
  (see recipe introduction)

Pour the soy sauce and sugar into a saucepan and simmer until the sugar has dissolved.

Add the vinegar, miso, and crushed sesame. Covered and kept in the fridge, it will last for 7 days.

Rosemary soy sauce dressing

This dressing is wonderful with meat; in fact it's a bit of a westernized flavor. But it's also great with Shabu shabu (see page 41).

Makes 1¼ cups [300 ml]
— 6 in [15 cm] sprig of rosemary
— 2 bay leaves
— 1¼ cups [300 ml] soy sauce
— 2 garlic cloves

Sterilize a jar: I usually fill it with boiling water, leave it for 3 or 4 minutes, then turn it upside down to remove the water and leave it on a clean cloth to dry out completely.

Place everything in the sterilized jar. Leave it in a cool, dark place for a minimum of 2 weeks and up to 4 months. It's now ready to use; there's no need to strain out the bits.

Perfect with beer dressing

This is my dad's recipe—every time he has a beer he has this dressing on his food! It's great for most summer dishes: salads, or anything you eat with salads, or even with sashimi.

Makes about 1¼ cups [300 ml]
— 1 apple
— ½ pear
— 1 onion
— 1 garlic clove
— ⅞ cup [200 ml] soy sauce
— ¼ cup [60 ml] sake or vodka
— 3 Tbsp brown sugar
— 2 Tbsp white miso
— 2 Tbsp sesame oil
— 2 Tbsp white sesame seeds, crushed
  (see page 19)
— 2 Tbsp whole white sesame seeds
— 1 Tbsp chili powder

Blend the apple, pear, onion, and garlic in a blender or food processor. Add the soy sauce and the sake and blend again.

Transfer to a saucepan, add the sugar and miso and set over low heat until the sauce thickens slightly.

Turn off the heat and add the sesame oil, crushed sesame, whole sesame seeds, and chili powder.

Let it cool and put it in a sterilized jar (see page 19) to keep in the fridge. It will keep for up to 4 weeks.

Lemon soy sauce dressing

My uncle found that vodka makes a good alternative to sake. Mirin is made from sake and sugar, and in the many places where sake is not available, vodka is a successful choice. My uncle, by the way, came across this substitution after many experimentations. Whisky, apparently, was an abject failure...

Makes about 1⅔ cups [400 ml] / Serves about 5
— Scant ⅔ cup [140 ml] sake or vodka
— ⅓ cup [60 g] superfine sugar
— Generous ⅓ cup [100 ml] lemon juice
— 200 ml [⅞ cup] soy sauce
— 5 cups [50 g] bonito flakes
— 1 x 4-in [10-cm] piece of dried kelp

Pour the sake and sugar into a saucepan and bring to a boil, then turn the heat off. Add all the other ingredients and set aside for four to six hours.

Strain the dressing into a bowl, pressing down on the bonito flakes to extract the maximum flavor. Covered, it will keep in the fridge for 1 month.

Shabu shabu dressing

This is a lighter dressing version of the heartier sauce (see page 41).

Makes enough for 2
— 2 Tbsp whole white sesame seeds
— 2 Tbsp white sesame seeds, crushed
  (see page 19)
— 2 Tbsp rice vinegar
— 3 Tbsp soy sauce
— 4 Tbsp hemp or grapeseed oil
— ½ onion, grated
— 2 in [1 thumb] ginger root, grated
— 1 garlic clove, crushed or grated
— 1 tsp sea salt

Put the whole sesame seeds, crushed sesame, vinegar, and soy sauce in a jar and mix well.

Add the oil and mix gently along with the onion, ginger, garlic, and salt.

Garden soy sauce dressing

This is very light and full of nutrition with a lot of vegetables inside it. It's nice with salad or—surprisingly—with beef.

Makes about 1¼ cups [300 ml] / Serves about 6
— 1 apple, grated
— 1 carrot, grated
— 1 onion, grated
— Generous ⅓ cup [100 ml] soy sauce
— Generous ⅓ cup [100 ml] rice vinegar
— 6½ Tbsp [80 g] honey or brown sugar

Simply mix all the ingredients together and it's ready to serve.

How to form sushi

In the Sushi chapter (see pages 100 to 121), you will need a little knowledge about how to form sushi rolls and nigiri. Neither of these are at all difficult, but these step-by-step guides will help you along.

Nigiri

Rub grapeseed oil or mayonnaise into your palms and fingers. Take 2½ Tbsp [20 g] of prepared sushi rice (see pages 104 and 110) in your right hand, if you are right-handed. (Or reverse all the instructions if you are left-handed.) Hold the shrimp (or other topping) in your left hand, across the base of your fingers.

Place the rice on top of the fish. Put your right index finger on top of the rice. Wrap your left hand around your right index finger, squeezing gently to make a nice shape. Turn your nigiri so the fish is on top, still placed over the base of the fingers.

Repeat the wrapping and squeezing steps to form a neat, compact piece of nigiri. Do not squash the rice together too hard; all movements should be gentle.

Now smooth the edges of the shrimp or other topping into an organic, graceful curve with no corners: the topping should drape elegantly over the rice.

Sushi rolls

Place a half sheet of nori near the bottom of a sushi rolling mat, rough side up and shiny side down. Place 1 heaping cup [150 g] of prepared sushi rice (see pages 104 and 110) in the middle. Spread it out gently with your fingers to form an even covering all over the seaweed, leaving a ⅜ in [1 cm] strip empty at the top edge. Place the filling in a straight line across the middle of the rice.

Gently slide both thumbs under the mat and rest your middle fingers on the filling. Lift the edge of the mat and seaweed nearest to you over the filling. Lift up the leading edge of the mat with your right hand, if you are right-handed. (Or simply reverse all the instructions if you are left-handed.) Roll, with your left hand supporting the roll. Pull gently on the mat with your right hand.

Gently squeeze the mat to form a tight roll. Remove the mat. With a very sharp knife, cut the roll in half. Put the halves together and cut into 6 pieces in total, wiping the blade between each cut.

Inside-out sushi rolls

Many of my Shoku-Iku sushi recipes have the rice on the outside and the seaweed in the center. To make these rolls, follow the instructions above, but after spreading out the rice, carefully flip over the whole piece, rice and seaweed, before adding the fillings.

SIMMER

"Adding flavors to simmering foods is a simple cooking technique, ideal when you want to create a one-pot meal."

Simmering is a very precise way of cooking, as heated water covers and surrounds food, maintaining a relatively constant temperature. This means the food cooks really evenly. It's a great choice for liquid-based dishes that contain a variety of ingredients, such as soups, stocks, and noodles.

One of the most frequent questions that I get asked as a chef is: how can you tell when water is simmering, rather than boiling? The technical answer is that the liquid is somewhere between 180 to 205°F [82 to 96°C]. For those without a thermometer, don't worry! The clues are also easy to see. A liquid for poaching should be flat and inactive, but a good simmering pan is slightly hotter. As a pan comes to a simmer you will be able to see small bubbles forming at the bottom and slowly rising to the top, but not aggressively or rapidly as you would see in a rolling boil.

This slow but gentle cooking technique helps to tenderize tougher cuts of meat. It is a gentler way to cook than boiling, so helps keep the food from breaking up, while the gradual nature of the process allows time for flavors to infuse and develop. More often than not, in my recipes, the simmering liquid will later form part of the dish. And as is the Shoku-Iku way, the cooking flavors are herb- and spice-based, so there's no need to load the simmering pan with salt prior to cooking.

JAPANESE CELLOPHANE NOODLE
(or vermicelli) **SOUP**

Cellophane noodles are made from potato and bean starch. This is very simple to make and filling, but easy for your body to digest. If you would like a vegetarian version, simply replace the tuna with shiitake mushrooms.

Serves 2 to 3

— **5 Iceberg lettuce leaves**
— **1 can of tuna in spring water, drained**
— **1 medium onion, finely sliced**
— **1 in [½ thumb] ginger root, finely sliced**
— **1 cup [50 g] Japanese cellophane noodles, or vermicelli**
— **Pinch of sea salt and freshly ground black pepper**
— **1 scallion, finely sliced**

Cut the lettuce and tuna into bite-sized pieces. Soak the onion slices in water for 15 minutes.

Bring 2⅛ cups [500 ml] water to a boil in a saucepan, add the lettuce, onion, and ginger and simmer for 3 to 4 minutes until the onion softens. Add the fish and noodles and simmer over medium heat for 2 or 3 minutes, until the noodles soften.

You may need to add some salt to flavor the soup, but taste and see; I like to add a pinch of ground black pepper.

Ladle into a bowl and sprinkle with the scallion.

RICE NOODLES WITH MUSHROOM BROTH

This is very filling and has all the vegetables within it. Again there's a very authentically Asian feel to this broth.

Serves 2

— **1 tsp kelp flakes**
— **Scant ½ cup [40 g] rice noodles**
— **4 shiitake mushrooms, finely sliced**
— **1 in [½ thumb] ginger root, grated**
— **1 tsp light soy sauce**
— **½ tsp sea salt**
— **½ tsp freshly ground black pepper**
— **½ tsp sesame oil**
— **1 tsp white sesame seeds**
— **1 scallion, sliced into julienne**
— **A little minced chile** (optional)

Pour 2½ cups [600 ml] water into a saucepan and bring to a boil.

Add the kelp flakes and rice noodles and simmer for 3 minutes, until the noodles soften.

Add the mushrooms, ginger, soy sauce, salt, and pepper, then turn the heat off and add the sesame oil, sesame seeds, and scallion.

Serve in bowls, adding some minced chile if you want a little spice.

DANCING SHRIMP

This is really rich in umami flavors and is very easy to make. The flavor of the shrimp mixes beautifully with those of the sesame oil and leek.

Serves 2 to 3

— ½ leek, sliced into julienne
— 5 oyster mushrooms, sliced ⅜ in [1 cm] thick
— 9 oz [250 g] large head-on shrimp
— 5 Tbsp sake or vodka
— 1 tsp sea salt
— 3 to 4 drops sesame oil
— 1 tsp soy sauce
— 1 scallion, sliced into julienne

Place the leek in a saucepan that has a lid. Lay the mushrooms on the bed of leek and the shrimp on top of those.

Add the sake, cover and cook over high heat until the sake starts to steam and the shrimps start to "dance" (as my grandmother used to say) in the liquid, then reduce the heat to medium so the pot is just simmering and add the salt, sesame oil, and soy sauce. Cover again and continue to simmer for 2 or 3 minutes.

Transfer to a serving plate and sprinkle with the scallion.

煮る Simmer

EDAMAME SOUP

When you add soy milk to a soup, it makes it thicker and more creamy.

Serves 2

— **1 Tbsp canola oil**
— **½ onion, minced**
— **7 oz [200 g] potato, finely chopped**
— **10½ oz [300 g] frozen edamame beans, defrosted**
— **Scant ½ cup [100 ml] soy milk**
— **Pinch of sea salt and freshly ground black pepper**
— **3 mint leaves, minced**

Pour the oil into a saucepan set over medium heat, add the onion and potato and cook until the onion softens. Add the edamame and 1⅞ cups [450 ml] water and simmer until the potato is tender.

Blend it into a smooth soup, then return it to the saucepan and add the soy milk. Return to a simmer and cook for 3 minutes. DO NOT boil it, or the soy milk could curdle.

Season, add the mint, and serve, warm or cold.

SPICY EDAMAME

Serve this as a side dish. It is a way to make the nutritional goodness of edamame a bit more sexy!

Serves 2

For the sauce
— **2 Tbsp light soy sauce**
— **1 garlic clove, grated**
— **1 in [½ thumb] ginger root, grated**
— **1 red or green chile, minced**
— **2 tsp mixed sesame seeds**
— **1½ Tbsp sesame oil**

For the edamame
— **1 tsp sea salt**
— **9 oz [250 g] frozen edamame beans, defrosted**

Mix all the ingredients for the sauce in a bowl.

Pour 8 cups [2 L] water into a saucepan and bring to a boil. Add the sea salt and edamame. Simmer for 3 minutes, then drain in a sieve.

Add the warm edamame to the sauce and mix with a spoon or your hands.

Serve immediately, as this is nicest when it's warm.

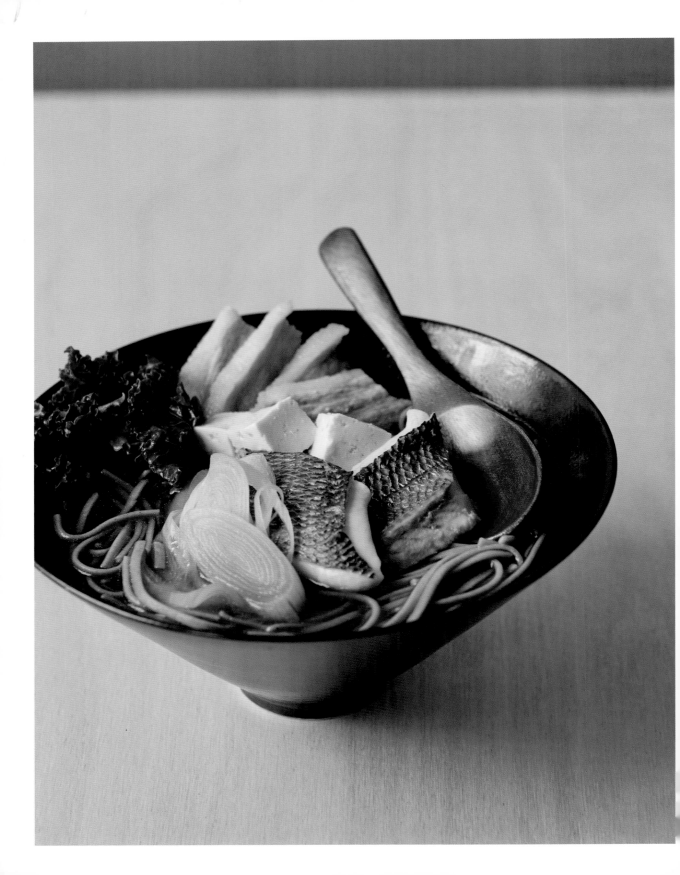

SOBA SOUP

This is an entrée. It is usually served in a tureen
on the table for people to help themselves into their
own small bowls, returning for seconds if they want.
Soba noodles are made from buckwheat, but many
also have wheat flour added, so check the package
if you are avoiding wheat.

Serves 2

— **9 oz [250 g] soba noodles**
— **5 Tbsp Noodle soup stock** (see page 18),
   plus more if needed
— **1 leek, finely sliced**
— **3½ oz [100 g] pork belly, cut into ¼ in
   [5 mm] thick slices**
— **½ sea bass fillet, cut into ¾ in [2 cm] slices**
— **6 oz [170 g] firm tofu, cut into ⅜ in
   [1 cm] pieces**
— **Handful of kale, cut into ⅜ in [1 cm] pieces**

Bring 8 cups [2 L] water to a boil in a large
saucepan. Add the noodles and cook for 4 to 5
minutes. Strain them through a sieve, reserving the
cooking liquid. Rinse the noodles under cold water.

Measure 4 cups [1 L] of the noodle cooking liquid and
return it to the rinsed-out saucepan set over medium
heat. Add the Noodle soup stock and return the
noodles. Add the leek, pork, sea bass, tofu, and kale,
cover and bring to a simmer.

Simmer for 2 to 3 minutes. Taste and see if you would
like to add more soup stock, then adjust the
seasonings accordingly and serve.

PAN TAI

In Japanese, "tai" is the word for sea bream.
So the name of this dish just means sea bream
cooked in a pan!

Serves 2

— 1 ¼ cups [240 g] brown rice
— 1 whole sea bream or sea bass,
   scaled and cleaned
— 2 tsp [5 g] finely sliced ginger root
— 1 ¼ cups [300 ml] Motoko dashi (see page 18)
— 1 chile, minced
— 1 quantity Everyday soy sauce dressing
   or Lemon soy sauce dressing
   (see pages 19 and 20)

Soak the brown rice in warm water for 30 minutes,
then drain. Preheat the broiler to its highest setting.

Lay the fish on a baking pan, dry it inside and out
with paper towels, then broil it on both sides until its
skin is a little brown.

Put the ginger, rice, and Motoko dashi in a large sauté
pan and lay the fish on top. Cover and cook over
medium heat for 6 to 7 minutes. Now reduce the
heat to low and simmer for another 15 minutes.

Increase the heat to high and cook for a final minute,
then turn off the heat completely and leave, still
covered, for 15 minutes.

Serve with the chile sprinkled on top and your choice
of soy sauce dressing.

CUCUMBER SOUP

This is best as a cold soup to serve in very warm weather, but you could also warm it up if you like. Use kelp instead of bonito for a vegetarian version.

Serves 2

— 1 cucumber, sliced into julienne
— ½ tsp grated garlic
— 1½ Tbsp superfine sugar
— ½ tsp sea salt
— ½ Tbsp bonito or kelp flakes
— 1 scallion, minced
— 1 Tbsp soy sauce
— Sea salt
— 2 Tbsp rice vinegar, or to taste
— 1 tsp white sesame seeds

Put the cucumber julienne in a bowl of ice-cold water and chill it in the fridge for 30 minutes.

Pour 1⅔ cups [400 ml] water into a saucepan and add the garlic, sugar, salt, and bonito flakes. Bring to a simmer, then leave to cool completely. Add the scallion and soy sauce, then season with salt and vinegar to taste.

Drain the cucumber and stir it into the soup, sprinkling the sesame seeds on top.

EGG AND TOFU DASHI SOUP

This could be a side dish or an entrée. It is elegant, with very subtle flavors.

Serves 2 to 3

For the soup base
— 1⅔ cups [400 ml] Basic dashi (see page 18)
— 1 tsp soy sauce
— ½ tsp sea salt
— 1 tsp sake or vodka

For the rest
— 12 oz [350 g] firm tofu, cut into ⅜ in [1 cm] pieces
— Large handful of baby spinach
— 3 eggs, lightly beaten
— 2 scallions, cut into 1¼ in [3 cm] slices on the diagonal

Add all the ingredients for the soup base to a saucepan and bring to a simmer. Add the tofu and return to a simmer. Add the spinach and pour in the beaten egg, slowly swirling it around with chopsticks. Increase the heat to medium and wait until the egg floats on top of the soup.

Serve in bowls sprinkled with the scallions.

GINGER SARDINES

Image on page 38

This is a classic dish, one that my grandma's generation would make often, because sardines have always been (and still are) cheap and very good for you.

Serves 2

— 8½ oz [240 g] sardines (4 fish), gutted and rinsed
— ⅓ cup [50 g] daikon, cut into ⅜ in [1 cm] semicircles
— 1 Tbsp honey
— 1 Tbsp mirin
— 1 Tbsp sake or vodka
— ½ Tbsp dashi flakes
— ⅜ in [1 cm] cube of dried kelp
— 1 in [½ thumb] ginger root, sliced into julienne
— 1 Tbsp soy sauce
— Pinch of superfine sugar

Put the sardines into a sauté pan with all the other ingredients.

Pour in a scant cup [200 ml] water and seal the pan with aluminum foil. Set over medium heat for 20 minutes, then serve.

VEGETABLE BROTH

Image on page 39

This is full of goodness, perfect for winter as it's so filling. If I have this at lunchtime, I can't eat dinner!

Serves 2 to 3

— 1 cup [30 g] dried shiitake mushrooms
— ½ cup [50 g] minced carrots
— ½ cup [50 g] minced onion
— 1 cup [50 g] thinly shredded leeks
— 1 cup [50 g] thinly shredded cabbage
— ⅓ cup [50 g] minced daikon
— 1½ cups [200 g] cooked Japanese short grain rice
— 2 Tbsp light soy sauce
— Pinch of sea salt
— 1 tsp mixed sesame seeds
— 1 tsp grated ginger root

Soak the shiitake mushrooms in 4 cups [1 L] warm water for 20 minutes, then strain into a bowl, pressing down on the mushrooms with a spoon and reserving the soaking liquid.

Add all the vegetables and mushrooms to a large saucepan, pouring in 2¼ cups [500 ml] of the shiitake soaking liquid (discard the gritty bit at the bottom). Set over medium heat and cook at a simmer for 15 to 20 minutes, until the carrots and daikon have softened.

Add the rice and return the broth to a simmer for 2 minutes.

Season with the soy sauce and salt, then ladle into bowls, sprinkling the sesame seeds and ginger on top.

SHABU SHABU

Use a medium casserole dish for this. The sauce
here is thicker than the other Shabu shabu dressing
in this book (see page 20). If you want a sauce that
is more like a light dressing, do feel free to use that
version instead. This one, though, is good to have with
the recipe when you are also going to be drinking
alcohol, at a party, say. It is meant as a feasting dish,
so do feel free to scale up the quantities if you want.
Tobanjan is a spicy paste; you can find it in Asian
shops or online and you really need it in this sauce.

Serves 2 to 3

— **1 leek, sliced into julienne**
— **1 whole lettuce, ripped into bite-sized pieces**
— **14 oz [400 g] wafer-thin sliced raw beef**
  (shabu shabu beef)

For the sauce
— **1 Tbsp brown sugar**
— **1 tsp grated ginger root**
— **1 tsp grated garlic**
— **½ Tbsp sesame oil**
— **½ Tbsp tobanjan**
— **1 Tbsp rice vinegar**
— **1 Tbsp soy sauce**
— **1 Tbsp white sesame seeds, crushed**
  (see page 19)
— **Generous 3 Tbsp [50 ml] oyster sauce**

First make the sauce. Dissolve the sugar
in 3 Tbsp hot water in a bowl, then add
all the other ingredients.

Pour 5 cups [1.2 L] water into a pan and bring
to a boil. Reduce the heat to a simmer and
add the leek. Cover and cook for 2 minutes.

Add the lettuce and 3 or 4 slices of beef,
moving the beef around in the hot liquid with
chopsticks and removing it once it's cooked.
Skim any residue that appears on the surface
of the water.

Serve the beef in small serving bowls, adding
the lettuce and leek. Serve with the sauce.

STEAM AND MICROWAVE

"Learn the art of steaming food
and you will get maximum nutrition
from everything you cook."

Steaming is a beautifully gentle way of cooking, which is why I choose it for so many of my recipes. It's a really popular way to prepare food in Japan. Because this cooking method doesn't require any fussing with—stirring, flipping or the like—it is particularly suited to fragile foods such as fish, which can break up easily. Vegetables, which have a tendency to become soggy when boiled, also fare much better with steam cooking, retaining more of their color and crispness. All of the Shoku-Iku goodness is preserved in steaming, as the food isn't submerged in liquid and therefore retains more of its nutrients. It's also a speedy way of cooking, as it takes only a short time to bring the steaming liquid up to temperature, unlike oven cooking where the oven can take time to heat up.

Steaming also keeps food succulently moist and incredibly fresh-tasting. Besides cooking the food, the steam itself allows me to infuse flavors into whatever I am preparing.

I always line my steamer bowls with circles of baking parchment to make it easy to lift the food off once it is cooked. If I'm using an open-topped container as a steaming basket, I cover the top with a piece of cheesecloth while the food cooks. This absorbs excess moisture, unlike a solid lid where the steam can collect and drip back onto the food.

You can use a microwave oven to produce a similar effect to steaming. Tightly plastic-wrap the items you want to cook before placing them in the microwave. This seals in the natural moisture and steam coming from the food and intensifies the flavors.

HEAVENLY STEAMED SEA BREAM

In Japan, and in some other food cultures, you sprinkle fish with sake and salt to get rid of "fishy" flavors and to improve the texture.

Serves 2

— ½ leek, sliced into julienne
— 1 sea bream or sea bass, skin slashed on both sides
— 2 Tbsp sake
— Pinch of sea salt
— 1 quantity Lemon soy sauce dressing (see page 20)

Place the leek and sea bream on a microwaveable dish. Sprinkle the sake and sea salt over both sides of the fish. Cover with plastic wrap, making sure it is well-sealed.

Using a 800 W oven, microwave for 4 or 5 minutes, until done. Open carefully, being cautious not to scald your hands in the steam.

Transfer to a serving plate and serve with the Lemon soy sauce dressing.

GLUTEN-FREE CHICKEN SAUSAGES

Both my son and my daughter are gluten-intolerant. They love sausages, but most of those you can buy contain gluten, so I started to make these at home and they are received enthusiastically.

Serves 2 to 3

— 2 skinless, boneless chicken breasts
— Pinch of sea salt and freshly ground black pepper
— 3 Tbsp [30 g] grated onion
— 1 egg, lightly beaten
— 1 Tbsp cornstarch
— handful of arugula leaves
— 1 quantity Perfect with beer sauce (see page 20)

Grind one of the chicken breasts in a blender or food processor. Slice the other chicken breast in half horizontally across its width and open it out.

Place a 10 in [25 cm] length of plastic wrap on the worktop and lay the opened chicken breast on top. Season it.

Mix the ground chicken with all the other ingredients except the arugula and Perfect with beer sauce and place the mixture on the chicken breast.

Roll the chicken breast up into a cylinder, wrapping the plastic wrap around it. Wrap in aluminum foil.

Set up a steamer and place the chicken sausage inside. Steam for 10 to 12 minutes. Leave it to cool down, then remove the foil and plastic wrap and slice into bite-sized pieces. Serve with arugula and Perfect with beer sauce.

SPICY STEAMED CHICKEN SALAD

Tobanjan is a seasoned chili sauce. It's very hot and you don't need a lot; even a small amount really does have quite a kick. Serve this chicken with a salad of shredded lettuce, cucumber, and scallion.

Serves 2

For the sauce
— 2 Tbsp soy sauce
— 1 Tbsp mirin
— 1 Tbsp superfine sugar
— 2 Tbsp sake or vodka
— 1 tsp tobanjan
— 1 tsp grated garlic
— 1 Tbsp white sesame seeds, crushed
  (see page 19)

For the chicken
— 10½ to 12 oz [300 to 350 g] skinless,
  boneless chicken thighs
— Pinch of sea salt
— 2 Tbsp sake or vodka
— 1 scallion, cut into 4 in [10 cm] strips

Mix all the ingredients for the sauce together in a large bowl.

Slice the chicken thighs horizontally to make them thinner and season with sea salt on both sides.

Place the chicken in a dish and add the sake and scallion. Turn to coat the chicken with the marinade, then set aside for 10 minutes.

Put the marinated chicken on a microwaveable pan, add the sauce and turn to coat again.

Wrap plastic wrap around the pan and seal it well. Using a 800 W oven, microwave for 5 minutes, then carefully open the plastic wrap (be careful not to scald your hands in the steam) and turn the contents over.

Seal with plastic wrap again and cook for another 2 to 3 minutes. Allow to cool to room temperature, then slice and serve with salad.

POSH DINNER IN 20 MINUTES

You can add a very little shredded sage to this, if you like. The cod is beautifully soft after steaming.

Serves 2

— 2 4-oz [120 g] cod fillets
— 2 Tbsp sake or white wine
— 4 cabbage leaves, cut into ⅜ in [1 cm] slices
— ¼ cup [30 g] carrots, finely sliced
— 4 frozen scallops, defrosted
— 2 Tbsp grapeseed oil
— 1 tsp yuzu juice or lemon juice
— Pinch of sea salt
— 1 quantity Everyday soy sauce dressing
  (see page 19)

Put the cod on a microwaveable pan and sprinkle with the sake. Leave for 15 minutes, then pat dry with paper towels.

Add the cabbage and carrot to the pan and sit the cod on the vegetables. Put the scallops on top and drizzle everything with the grapeseed oil and yuzu juice, sprinkling with sea salt.

Cover with plastic wrap. Using a 800 W oven, microwave for 4 minutes, then leave, still wrapped in plastic wrap, for another 4 minutes. Carefully unwrap (be careful not to scald your hands in the steam).

Serve with Everyday soy sauce dressing.

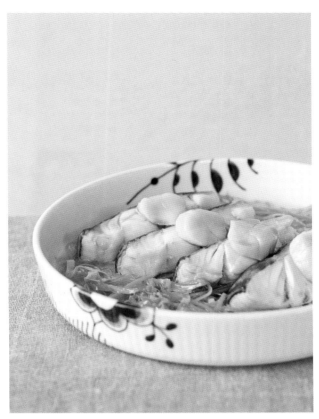

GINGER CHICKEN WITH BEANSPROUTS

This is incredibly easy to make—anybody could tackle it—and very delicious.

Serves 2 to 3

— 10½ oz [300 g] skinless, boneless chicken
  thighs, cut into bite-sized pieces
— ½ onion, grated
— 1 garlic clove, finely sliced
— 1 in [½ thumb] ginger root, finely grated
— 6 Tbsp sake or white wine
— 2 Tbsp soy sauce
— Pinch of freshly ground black pepper
— Large handful of beansprouts
— 3 to 4 cilantro leaves

Put the chicken in a plastic food bag with all the other ingredients except the beansprouts and cilantro. Massage to cover the meat with all the flavorings and leave in the fridge for 1 hour.

Place a nonstick frying pan over medium heat and put in the chicken and sauce. Cook until the chicken is browned, then add the beansprouts, cover and steam for an additional 3 or 4 minutes. Serve sprinkled with the cilantro.

SHRIMP PILLOW

This is very nice, with lots of lovely textures. It's essentially a very easy homemade dumpling. This is gluten-free as I use rice paper wrappers instead of wheat-based spring roll wrappers. I first made these for my gluten-intolerant son and he loves them.

Makes 10

— 7 oz [200 g] ground turkey or chicken
— 6 in [15 cm] length of leek, minced
— 1½ Tbsp sake or vodka
— ½ tsp sea salt
— Pinch of freshly ground black pepper
— 10 large rice paper sheets
— 20 large cooked shrimp, deveined
  if necessary
— Couple of handfuls of frozen edamame
  beans, defrosted
— 1 quantity Everyday soy sauce dressing
  or Lemon soy sauce dressing
  (see pages 19 and 20)

Put the ground turkey, leek, sake, sea salt, and pepper into a bowl and mix well.

Place a rice paper sheet in a shallow dish of warm water for 10 to 15 seconds, to soften. Shake it gently to get rid of excess water and place on a large plate.

Spoon 1 Tbsp of the turkey mixture onto the middle of the sheet and add two shrimp and a few edamame beans. Fold it into a rectangle as if you were wrapping a present. Repeat to use all the filling and rice papers.

Line a steamer with baking parchment. Place all the shrimp pillows next to each other in the steamer, making sure the parcels do not touch.

Steam for 5 to 6 minutes, or until the parcels themselves are steaming.

Take out of the steamer and serve with your choice of soy sauce dressing.

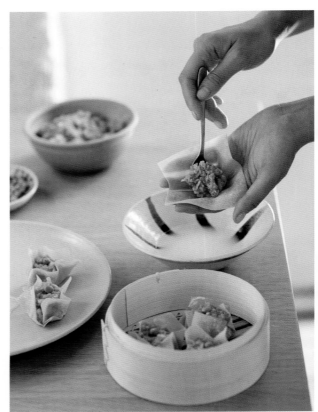

STUFFED VEGETABLES

This is full of protein from the beans. When we have dishes that contain lots of protein but no meat, we call it "meat of the garden!" But, if you do want some meat, this dish is nice with pork. It's also a good dish for sneaking lots of vegetables into recalcitrant children.

Serves 4

For the peppers and filling
— **2 tomatoes**
— **1 eggplant, cut into ⅜ in [1 cm] cubes and soaked in water for 30 minutes**
— **14 oz [400 g] canned soybeans or black-eyed peas, drained and rinsed**
— **Sea salt and freshly ground black pepper**
— **1 green chile, seeded and finely chopped**
— **2 green bell peppers, tops cut off and reserved**
— **2 red bell peppers, tops cut off and reserved**
— **1 quantity Shabu shabu dressing,** (see page 20)

For the paste
— **1 tsp white miso paste**
— **1 Tbsp mirin**
— **1 Tbsp sake or vodka**

Cut a cross at the base of the tomatoes and put them in a bowl of boiling water for 1 minute. Remove, peel off the skin and cut into ⅜ in [1 cm] cubes.

Preheat the broiler to its highest setting. Drain the eggplant and broil both eggplant and tomatoes on both sides for 2 to 3 minutes until lightly brown. Mix with the beans.

Mix together all the ingredients for the paste and stir into the eggplant mixture, seasoning to taste, and adding the chile.

Stuff the mixture into the peppers. Put on a large microwaveable pan and seal with plastic wrap. Using a 800 W oven, microwave for 4 minutes then leave, still covered with the plastic wrap, for 2 minutes. Unwrap, being careful not to scald your hands.

If you would like a chargrilled finish, pop them under a hot broiler until burnished. Serve with Shabu shabu dressing.

BRITISH PORK DUMPLINGS

I've called this recipe "British" because it mixes apple with the pork filling. My children love the combination, so I invented this dumpling and it was a big hit.

Makes 20

For the filling
— **7 oz [200 g] ground pork**
— **½ medium onion, minced**
— **2 cabbage leaves, minced**
— **½ apple, peeled and grated**
— **1 Tbsp superfine sugar**
— **1 Tbsp sesame oil**
— **1 Tbsp grated ginger root**
— **1 Tbsp sake or vodka**
— **1 Tbsp light soy sauce**
— **1 Tbsp cornstarch**

For the dumplings
— **20 wonton sheets**
— **1 tsp cornstarch**
— **20 green peas**
— **A little flavorless vegetable oil, to brush**
— **1 quantity Everyday soy sauce dressing or Shabu shabu dressing** (see pages 19 and 20)

Mix all the filling ingredients, except the cornstarch, in a bowl and set aside for 10 minutes. Add the cornstarch and mix well again.

Hold a wonton sheet in your hand and put 1 to 1½ Tbsp of filling into the center of the sheet. Mix the 1 tsp cornstarch in a cup with 5 Tbsp of water. Use this paste to moisten the sheet around the filling. Close your hand to mold the wonton into a ball shape, leaving the top open to expose the filling.

Push one green pea into the top of the filling.

Line a steamer with baking parchment. Brush a little oil under each dumpling and place them in the steamer, making sure they don't touch each other. Put the lid on and steam for 5 to 7 minutes until cooked.

Serve with Shabu shabu dressing or Everyday soy sauce dressing.

BACON AND CABBAGE STEAMED PUDDING

You need to make this in a bowl, so you can build up a round shape; it should be like a cake or a pudding that you can cut into wedges to serve.

Serves 2 to 3

— **10 cabbage leaves, ribs removed**
— **10 slices unsmoked bacon**

Begin layering the cabbage and bacon in a medium microwaveable bowl. Start with a cabbage leaf first. Fill to the top. Push everything down to make sure it is tightly pressed together.

Plastic wrap the top to seal it well.

Using a 800 W oven, microwave for 3 to 4 minutes, until the bacon is cooked. Leave the bowl with the plastic wrap still on for another 5 minutes.

Remove the plastic wrap (be careful not to scald your hands in the steam) and place a large plate upside down on top of the bowl.

Transfer to the plate and leave it for few seconds to make sure the cabbage and bacon are released. Cut into wedges like a cake to serve.

"FULL JAPANESE" GARDEN BREAKFAST

This is a quick, easy way of having eggs for breakfast. I always like to eat some greens at breakfast as well, as did all my family before me. This is a fusion of British and Japanese cooking methods and flavors —why not? I'm Japanese and I live in Britain—so I call it a "full Japanese." Use a lidded sauté pan.

Serves 2

— **1 tsp canola oil**
— **1 garlic clove, grated**
— **Large handful of kale, chopped into ⅜ in [1 cm] slices**
— **Handful of baby spinach leaves**
— **3 cherry tomatoes, quartered**
— **3 shiitake mushrooms, finely sliced**
— **3 white mushrooms, finely sliced**
— **4 eggs**
— **1 quantity Garden soy sauce dressing** (see page 20)
— **A little minced chile** (optional)

Heat the oil in a sauté pan over medium heat, add the garlic and stir until fragrant.

Add the kale with any water from washing still clinging to its leaves, the spinach, tomatoes, and mushrooms and cook until almost tender.

Hollow out four spaces and drop an egg into each. Put the lid on and cook over low heat to steam for 3 to 4 minutes, depending on how you like your eggs (we only cooked two for the photo).

Transfer to plates and serve with Garden soy sauce dressing, sprinkled with chile, if you want.

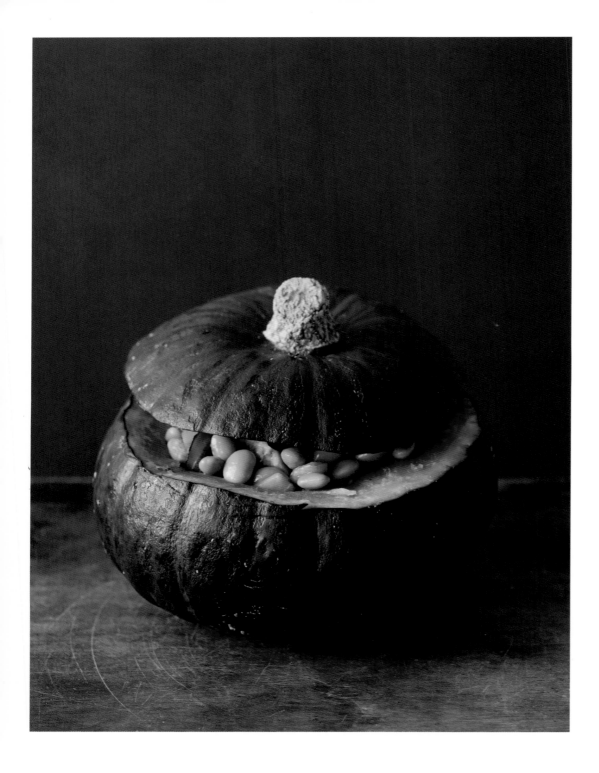

SQUASH OF PLENTY!

This is a Japanese monk vegan recipe. It is rich in umami and utterly delicious, with the soft, sweet pumpkin and tofu, but with a fresh, simple flavor. Use a round green squash with bright orange insides: Crown Prince is good.

Serves 3 to 4

— 1 small kabocha, about 6 in [15 cm] in diameter
— 1 Tbsp sesame oil
— ¼ cup [30 g] carrots, cut into ⅜ in [1 cm] strips
— 2 shiitake mushrooms, finely sliced
— 2 heaping Tbsp [20 g] frozen edamame beans, defrosted
— Sea salt
— 12 oz [350 g] firm tofu, drained and dried with paper towels
— 2 Tbsp white sesame seeds, crushed (see page 19)
— 1 Tbsp cornstarch

Sauce
— 1⅔ cups [400 ml] Basic dashi (see page 18)
— 2 Tbsp mirin
— 2 Tbsp light soy sauce
— 2 Tbsp cornstarch

Cut a 1¼ in [3 cm] lid off the top of the kabocha. Remove the kabocha seeds.

In a large steamer, steam the whole kabocha with its lid for 15 minutes.

Meanwhile, heat a pan over medium heat and add the sesame oil. Stir-fry the carrots, mushrooms, and edamame for 3 minutes, seasoning with sea salt. Break the tofu into chunks and add them, too.

Add the crushed sesame seeds and cornstarch and mix well until the carrots soften. Spoon the tofu and vegetable mix into the kabocha and steam for another 10 minutes.

Meanwhile, heat a pan over medium heat and add the dashi, mirin, and soy sauce. Separately mix the cornstarch with 5 Tbsp water, add to the pan, and stir well until it thickens.

Remove the kabocha lid and pour in the sauce. Serve.

CHICKEN LEMON POT

This steamed dish is very healthy, and like most steamed dishes, retains a lot of its nutrition. The flavor is very fresh and energizing.

Serves 3 to 4

— 1¾ lb [800 g] daikon, peeled and grated
— 5 Napa cabbage leaves, cut into slices 2 in [5 cm] thick
— 18 oz [500 g] skinless, boneless chicken thighs, cut into slices ⅜ in [1 cm] thick
— 1 lemon, cut into slices ⅛ in [4 mm] thick
— 1 Tbsp dashi flakes (or 3 generous Tbsp [50 ml] Motoko dashi, see page 18)
— 1 quantity Everyday soy sauce dressing or Lemon soy sauce dressing (see pages 19 and 20)

Lay the grated daikon in an even layer in a cast-iron saucepan or casserole dish. Lay the Napa cabbage, chicken, and lemon on top, in that order.

Add the dashi flakes or Motoko dashi.

Cover and set the saucepan over medium heat for 6 to 7 minutes, or until you see steam coming out, then reduce the heat to low and cook for another 4 or 5 minutes. Turn the heat off completely and leave for a final 5 minutes.

Serve with your choice of soy sauce dressing.

DAIKON STEAK

Steamed daikon has quite a bland taste, subtler than that of western radishes. This makes a good entrée when served with miso soup.

Serves 2

— 12 oz [350 g] daikon, peeled and cut into slices ¾ in [2 cm] thick
— 1 quantity Perfect with beer sauce (see page 20)

Place the daikon slices in a microwaveable pan, next to, but not on top of each other. Add 2 Tbsp water and seal with plastic wrap.

Using a 800 W oven, microwave for 5 to 7 minutes then leave, still covered, for another 3 minutes. Unwrap, being careful not to scald your hands in the steam.

Serve with Perfect with beer sauce.

STEAMED STICKY RICE

If I'm making this at home with my children, I need to double the recipe, because they love it so much. It is pretty addictive... Leave out the chicken for a vegetarian version.

Serves 4 to 6

— 1 Tbsp canola oil
— 3½ oz [100 g] skinless, boneless chicken thighs, cut into ⅜ in [1 cm] cubes (optional)
— 4 shiitake mushrooms, finely sliced
— ½ cup [60 g] carrots, sliced into julienne
— Scant 2 oz [50 g] artichoke, finely sliced or shredded
— 4 oyster mushrooms, finely sliced
— 1 head of enoki mushrooms, broken into pieces
— 4 Tbsp sake or vodka
— 3 Tbsp light soy sauce
— 3 Tbsp mirin
— 1 Tbsp superfine sugar
— 2 Tbsp kelp flakes
— 1 lb [450 g] Japanese glutinous rice (mochigome)
— 1 scallion, minced (optional)
— sprinkling of white sesame seeds (optional)

Heat the canola oil in a sauté pan set over medium heat and cook the chicken (if using), turning, until lightly brown.

Add all the vegetables and seasonings and continue to cook, stirring well, until the vegetables are tender.

Meanwhile, line a steamer with cheesecloth, add the rice and steam over high heat for 30 to 35 minutes.

When the rice is ready, put it in a bowl with the vegetables and mix well.

Return the mixture to the cloth-lined steamer and cook for another 15 minutes over high heat. Now turn off the heat and leave, still covered, for a final 10 minutes. Serve sprinkled with either scallion or sesame seeds.

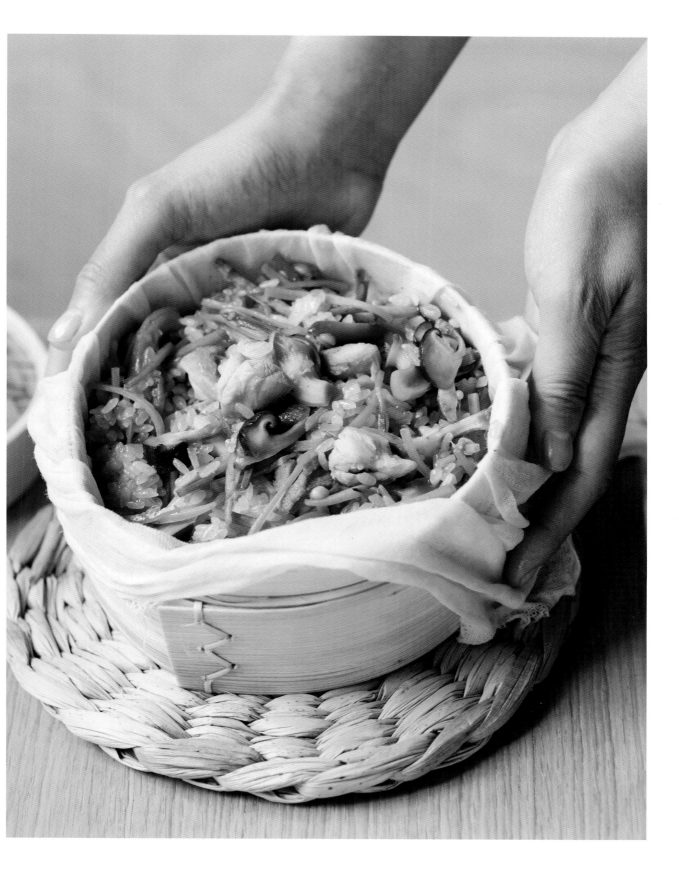

HOT STEAMED CHICKEN

This is very light, super-easy to make, and has an authentically Asian taste to it. It's a typical dish you might see at a Japanese dinner table.

Serves 2 to 3

— 18 oz [500 g] skinless, boneless chicken thighs, cut into ⅝ in [1.5 cm] pieces
— 1 Tbsp sea salt
— 2 Tbsp sesame oil
— 2 Tbsp cornstarch
— 1 Tbsp chicken stock
— 1 Tbsp soy sauce
— 1 Tbsp sake or vodka
— 1 Tbsp oyster sauce
— 1 garlic clove, minced
— 1 scallion, minced

Put the chicken in a bowl and add the sea salt and sesame oil. Stir so all the meat is coated and leave to marinate for 15 minutes. Stir in the cornstarch.

Pour ⅔ cup [150 ml] water into a saucepan and add the stock, soy sauce, sake, and oyster sauce. Bring to a boil, then remove from the heat.

Set up a steamer. Put the chicken into a heatproof dish and add the sauce. Sprinkle evenly with the garlic and steam for 20 minutes. Sprinkle with scallion and serve.

JAPANESE GARDEN (gluten-free)

This dish was originally a Japanese monk recipe, a vegan dish. I tweaked it... and added bacon! I'm not sure the monks would approve. You can, of course, leave out the bacon.

Serves 2 to 3

— 7 oz [200 g] pumpkin, cut into ⅜ in [1 cm} cubes
— 7 oz [200 g] turnips, quartered if large, left whole if tiny
— 5¼ oz/1 cup [150 g] daikon], cut into ⅜ in [1cm] semicircles
— 3 slices bacon
— 7 oz [200 g] broccoli, cut into ¾ in [2 cm] pieces
— 1 heaping cup [100 g] snow peas

For the sauce
— 2 Tbsp balsamic vinegar
— 1 tsp honey
— 1 Tbsp soy sauce
— 1 tsp sesame oil
— 1 tsp white sesame seeds, crushed (see page 19)
— Pinch of sea salt

Place the pumpkin, turnips, and daikon into a large steamer, cover the top with the bacon slices and cook for 6 minutes.

Add the broccoli and snow peas and cook for another 3 minutes.

Meanwhile, mix all the ingredients for the sauce.

Transfer the vegetables and bacon to a serving plate and sprinkle over the sauce.

JAPANESE SOUFFLÉ

The texture of this is soft; much softer than a western soufflé. You will need two medium-sized china cups. There's a bit of everything in this version, but leave out the chicken and shrimp if you prefer.

Serves 2

— **2¼ cups [500 ml] Basic dashi** (see page 18)
— **1 Tbsp mirin**
— **½ tsp soy sauce**
— **1 tsp sea salt**
— **3 eggs, lightly beaten**
— **1¾ oz [50 g] chicken breast, cut into ⅜ in [1 cm] pieces**
— **2 to 3 shiitake mushrooms, finely sliced**
— **2 small cooked shrimp, deveined if necessary**
— **4 cilantro leaves**

Pour the dashi, mirin, and soy sauce in a bowl, add the salt and mix well. Add the eggs, then strain through a sieve to make sure the mixture is smooth.

Divide the chicken, mushrooms, and shrimp between two china cups and add the egg mixture; it should fill each cup by about two-thirds.

Place the cups in a steamer set over medium heat and cook for 10 minutes, then reduce the heat to low and steam for another 10 minutes. Turn the heat off. Leave the cups in the steamer for a final 5 minutes. (If you don't have a steamer, place the cups in a deep saucepan containing ¾ in [2 cm] of boiling water and cook, using the same timings.)

Sprinkle each cup with cilantro and serve warm.

SWEET SOY SAUCE MOCHI

Mochi (pronounced "mow-chee") is an authentic, classic Japanese dessert. The texture inside is very soft, almost silky.

Serves 4

For the mochi
— **1⅛ cups [150 g] rice flour**

For the sauce
— **2 Tbsp soy sauce**
— **2 Tbsp superfine sugar**
— **1 Tbsp cornstarch**

Soak four bamboo skewers in a dish of water.

Put the rice flour into a large bowl and gradually pour in ⅔ cup [150 ml] warm water, stirring with a wooden spoon. Knead the dough with your hands for 2 to 3 minutes.

Lay a damp cloth into a steamer.

Cut the mochi dough into ¾ in [2 cm] balls—or any shapes really—and lay them on top, then steam over high heat for 15 minutes. This is just to cook the mixture through and they won't remain in the shapes they hold at this stage, so don't waste time shaping them!

Remove the mochi balls from the steamer and place on a sheet of wax paper. Hold the sides of the wax paper, bringing the dough balls together. Massage through the paper well until the dough feels soft and fleshy. Cut the mass into 12 pieces, roll each into a ball and put three balls on each skewer.

Preheat the broiler to its highest setting. Put aluminum foil around the exposed parts of the skewers and broil for 2 minutes on each side.

Meanwhile, make the sauce. Put all the ingredients into a small saucepan with a scant ½ cup [100 ml] water and cook over medium heat. When it's bubbling, mix well with a wooden spoon, turning the heat off once it has become clearer and thicker.

Serve on top of the mochi.

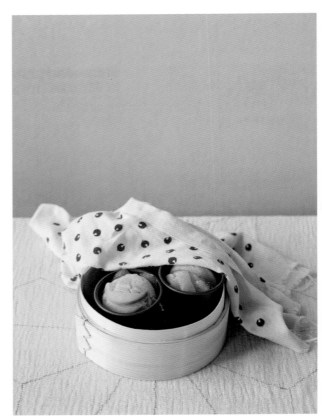

SWEET POTATO TREAT

You can eat this as a snack, a dessert, or a side dish. You can also cool the mixture and wrap it in puff pastry, forming a triangle of pastry around the filling. You could cook it under a medium broiler, turning to cook both sides. Though delicious, that, of course, would be far less Shoku-Iku and far more western...

Serves 3 to 4

— 14 oz [400 g] sweet potato, peeled and cut into slices ¼ in [5 mm] thick
— 2 apples, peeled and cut into slices ⅜ in [1 cm] thick
— ⅓ cup [80 ml] sake or vodka
— 5 tsp [25 g] honey
— 1½ tsp sea salt

Place the sweet potato slices in a saucepan, laying them next to each other, then place the apple slices on top.

Pour in 1 scant cup [200 ml] water and add the sake, honey, and sea salt. Set over high heat and cook until you see steam coming out of the pan, then reduce the heat to medium and steam for another 4 to 5 minutes until all the liquid has been absorbed.

FRUIT BUNS

This is a great snack for lunch or between meals. I also put it in lunch boxes. It's really easy to make.

Makes 6 to 7

— ½ tsp sea salt
— 1 tsp baking powder
— 3¼ Tbsp [40 g] superfine sugar
— 1⅛ cups [150 g] plain flour (or gluten-free flour)
— 5 oranges, peeled and sliced
— 2 apples, finely sliced
— 10 raisins

Pour ⅔ cup [150 ml] room temperature water into a bowl and add the salt, baking powder, and sugar. Now stir in the flour.

Divide between 6 or 7 x 1½-in [4-cm] wide heatproof pudding cups, or muffin pans, arranging orange, apple and/or raisins on top on each.

Put the pudding cups on a steamer rack, cover with a cloth instead of a lid, to absorb the water, then steam for 15 minutes.

BROIL, GRILL, AND FRY

"Intensify the natural flavors
of your food with the flashing
heat of a broiler."

Grilling is such a clean way to cook, as it doesn't need to involve oils as frying does (even if you are frying a low-fat foodstuff, it will always pick up the oils from the pan). And of course when grilling, any excess fats in food will drip off, lowering its fatty content. In this chapter, "grilling" can mean broiling under a heat source, or griddling in a pan.

Remember, when grilling or frying meats, to always allow a resting period. As tempting as the food may smell, let it sit for a few minutes. This allows the juices in the meat to permeate back through it and not flood out when cut. It also improves the texture, by allowing the fibers to relax and soften.

Grilling or frying also adds to the flavor of your food. Any natural sugars in vegetables will caramelize slightly, making them irresistible with very little effort. I use plenty of marinades when grilling and frying and again the taste is amplified, as the flavors heat and bubble under a hot broiler or in a hot pan.

Cooking vegetables this way keeps more of the vitamins and nutrients than other cooking methods, such as boiling. I also find that my children are less resistant to vegetables when they are grilled or fried.

This chapter gives me a chance to experiment with things you wouldn't normally associate with grilling or frying. My Full of goodness recipe (see page 75) is incredibly speedy to make, as you are broiling pumpkin. The key is to slice the pumpkin nice and thinly so it becomes succulent under the broiler quickly. My mother is a fan of lightly broiled avocado strips (see page 75). And of course you can toast nuts and seeds just as easily under the broiler rather than fry them.

JAPANESE BURGER

This recipe is perfect for my three children. The tofu makes the burger light and more digestion-friendly, as it has soy protein rather than just all meat.

Makes 3 to 4 burgers

For the burgers
— 3½ oz [100 g] tofu
— 3½ oz [100 g] ground turkey
— 1 tsp grated garlic
— 1 egg, lightly beaten
— ½ onion, grated
— Sea salt
— ¾ cup [100 g] canned chickpeas, mashed
— ½ Tbsp sesame oil

For the bean salad
— 2 Tbsp canola oil
— 8 oz [225 g] canned adzuki beans, drained and rinsed
— 2 shallots, finely chopped
— 10 green beans, chopped into ¼ in [5 mm] lengths
— 2 tomatoes, finely chopped
— 3 Tbsp balsamic vinegar
— ½ tsp chili powder

To serve
— 4 Tbsp [30 g] grated daikon
— 4 rocket salad , or cilantro leaves, shredded
— ¼ lemon

Pat the tofu dry with paper towels, then place in a microwaveable bowl, seal with plastic wrap and using a 800 W oven, microwave for 5 minutes. Leave, covered, for another 3 minutes.

Add to a bowl with the turkey, garlic, egg, onion, sea salt, and chickpeas and mix well. Leave it for 10 minutes to settle.

Take ⅓ to ¼ of the mixture in your hands and shape it into a burger. Squeeze it lightly to make sure there is no air in the meat. Repeat to make 3 or 4 burgers.

Heat a nonstick pan over medium heat and add the sesame oil. Place the burgers in the pan and fry for 3 to 4 minutes on each side.

Add 2 Tbsp water to the pan and put the lid on. Cook for another few minutes, until the water has evaporated.

Meanwhile, make the bean salad. Heat a pan over medium heat and add the canola oil. Add the adzuki beans and shallots and fry until the shallots soften. Turn the heat off and let cool. (I usually take them out of the pan to cool.)

Put the green beans in a microwaveable pan and add 1 Tbsp water. Seal it well with plastic wrap. Cook in the microwave for 3 minutes then leave, covered, for another 3 minutes. Remove from the pan and leave to cool.

Put the tomatoes in a bowl and add the green beans, adzuki bean mixture, balsamic vinegar, and chili powder.

Mix the grated daikon and rocket well. Serve the burger with grated daikon and rocket on top, with a pile of bean salad. Squeeze a little bit of lemon juice on top of the daikon.

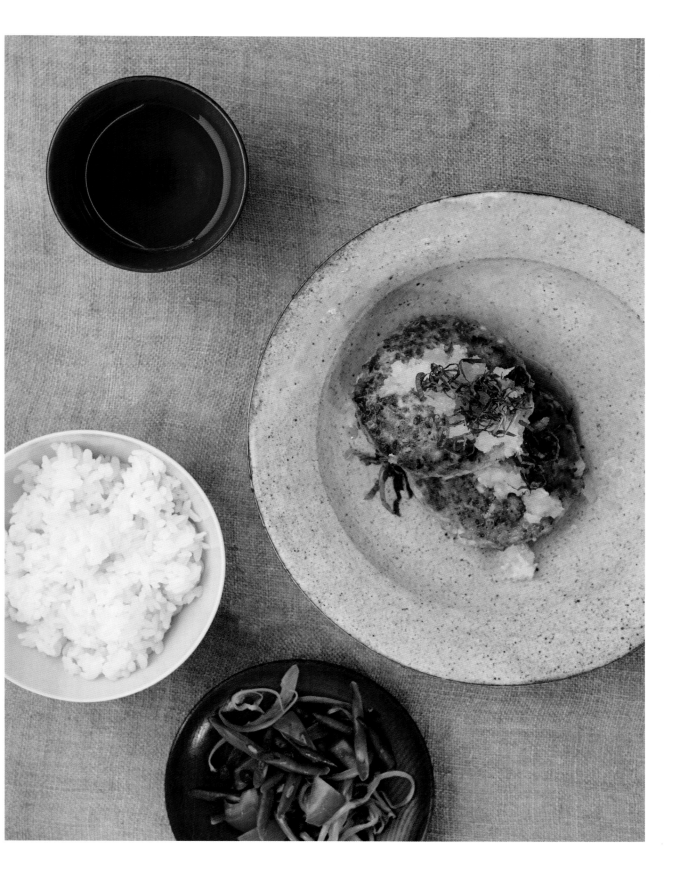

SHRIMP BARBECUE

These shrimp have a great flavor balance between the lemon and the garlic. Despite containing no hot spices, this dish nevertheless gives a bit of a kick.

Serves 3

— **2 Tbsp grapeseed oil**
— **1 Tbsp sake or vodka**
— **1 tsp grated garlic**
— **⅓ cup [75 ml] lemon juice, plus lemon wedges to serve** (optional)
— **½ tsp freshly ground white pepper**
— **1 tsp sea salt**
— **15 tiger shrimp, heads removed, shelled and deveined**
— **5 scallions, sliced into julienne**

Put the grapeseed oil, sake, garlic, lemon juice, pepper and salt in a plastic food bag, add the shrimp, close the bag, and massage to coat. Leave for 2 hours in the fridge. If you want to serve them on bamboo skewers, soak the skewers for at least 30 minutes, so they don't catch fire in the pan.

When you're ready to cook, you can thread the shrimps onto bamboo skewers. Otherwise, just cook them as they are.

Place a large frying pan over medium heat and allow to get hot. Add the shrimp and their marinade and cook for 2 minutes on each side.

Transfer the shrimp and sauce to a serving dish and sprinkle with the scallions. Serve with lemon wedges, if you like.

JAPANESE GRILLED VEGETABLE "STIR-FRY"

This is a dish completely without oil, that is half-grilled and half-steamed to give satisfying umami flavors. You can taste the vegetables in it rather than just soy sauce, black bean sauce, or oyster sauce, which can be the case in traditional stir-fries.

Serves 2

— 7 oz [200 g] beansprouts, preferably fresh
— 2 large handfuls [100 g] baby spinach
— ½ to ⅔ cup [60 to 80 g] very finely sliced carrots
— 6–8 asparagus spears
— Sea salt and freshly ground black pepper
— 1 quantity Everyday soy sauce dressing or Lemon soy sauce dressing
  (see pages 19 and 20)
— white sesame seeds, to serve

Place all the vegetables in a microwaveable pan, add 1 Tbsp water and seal with plastic wrap.

Using a 800 W oven, microwave for 4 minutes, then leave, covered, for another 2 minutes. Remove the plastic wrap, being careful not to scald your hands.

Heat a frying or griddle pan on high heat and grill the asparagus and carrots quickly without any oil until lightly browned on both sides. (This depends on how you like it. I like asparagus lightly charred.)

Put the beansprouts, spinach, carrots, and asparagus in a bowl and mix well.

Season with sea salt and pepper. Serve with your choice of soy sauce dressing and sprinkle with white sesame seeds.

EGGPLANT AND SHALLOT SALAD

This could either make an entrée or a side dish, depending on what you prefer.

Serves 2

— 7 small shallots, peeled and finely sliced
— 1 eggplant, cut into 4, then sliced into ½-in [1-cm] pieces
— 2 to 3 Tbsp Lemon soy sauce dressing
  (see page 20)

Soak the shallot slices in water for 10 minutes, then drain.

Preheat the broiler to its highest setting. Put the eggplant in a grill pan and grill on both sides until it is brown.

Mix the eggplant and shallots well in a bowl and add the Lemon soy sauce dressing.

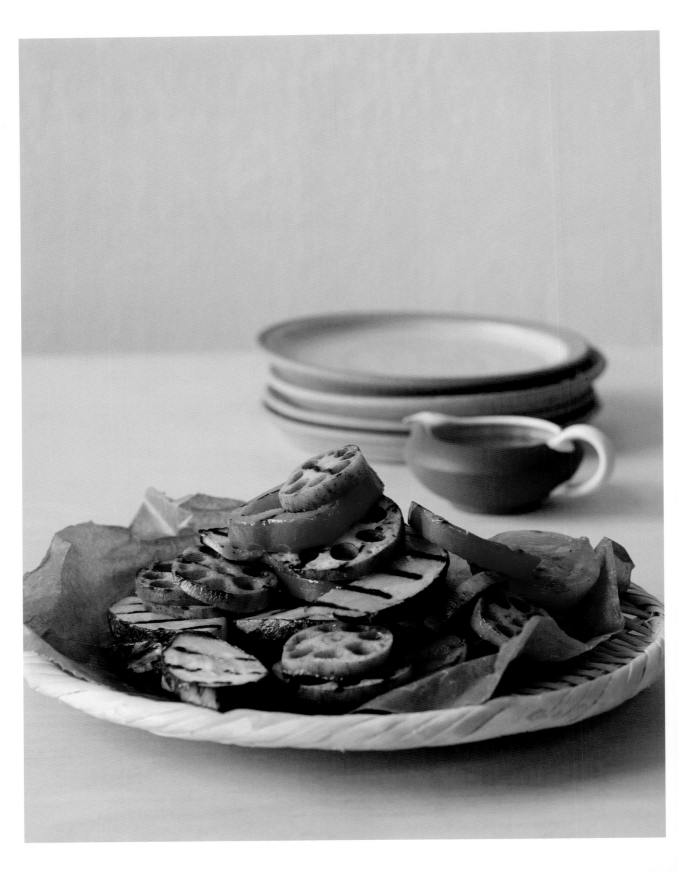

FULL OF GOODNESS

We eat this as a main dish. There are lots of different colors in it, which means you eat it with your eyes as well as with your palate.

Serves 2 to 3

For the vegetables
— 2 tomatoes, cut into ¼ in [5 mm] slices
— 1 zucchini, cut into ¼ in [5 mm] slices
— 1 red bell pepper, cut into ¼ in [5 mm] slices
— 1 yellow bell pepper, cut into ¼ in [5 mm] slices
— 1½ oz [40 g] lotus root, cut into ¼ in [5 mm] slices
— ⅓ cup [40 g] pumpkin, cut into ¼ in [5 mm] slices

For the sauce
— 3 cups [30 g] bonito flakes
— 2 Tbsp soy sauce
— 2 Tbsp rice vinegar
— 2 Tbsp canola or grapeseed oil
— Pinch of sea salt
— Pinch of superfine sugar

Preheat the broiler to its highest setting, or heat a griddle pan. Place all the vegetables on a pan and grill both sides for 3 to 4 minutes, or for longer if you like a little smoky flavor. Use the griddle pan if you want griddle marks.

Meanwhile, make the sauce. Pour 1 scant cup [200 ml] hot water into a cup and add the bonito flakes. Leave for 5 minutes. Add the rest of the ingredients and mix well.

Transfer the vegetables to a serving plate and pour over the sauce. Serve immediately.

BROILED AVOCADO

The texture of a broiled avocado is creamy and sort of buttery. Me and my mom tried broiling avocado one day as an experiment. We wanted to see if you could use it for anything other than salads. And you can!

Serves 4 as a side dish

— 3 fingers of okra
— 2 avocados
— 4 cherry tomatoes, quartered
— prinkling of dried seaweed

For the sauce
— ¾ cup [7 g] bonito flakes
— 2 umeboshi (salted plums), pitted and mashed
— ½ tsp wasabi paste
— ½ tsp soy sauce
— 1 tsp mirin

Boil the okra fingers for 2 minutes, until tender, then drain and cut into ¼ in [5 mm] slices.

Preheat the broiler to its highest setting. Cut the avocados in half, remove the pits, peel, and slice. Broil, turning, until browned. Cut into cubes.

Put the avocados, okra, and tomatoes in a bowl.

Separately, mix all the ingredients for the sauce. Add the sauce to the vegetables and mix well.

Serve in small bowls and sprinkle seaweed on top.

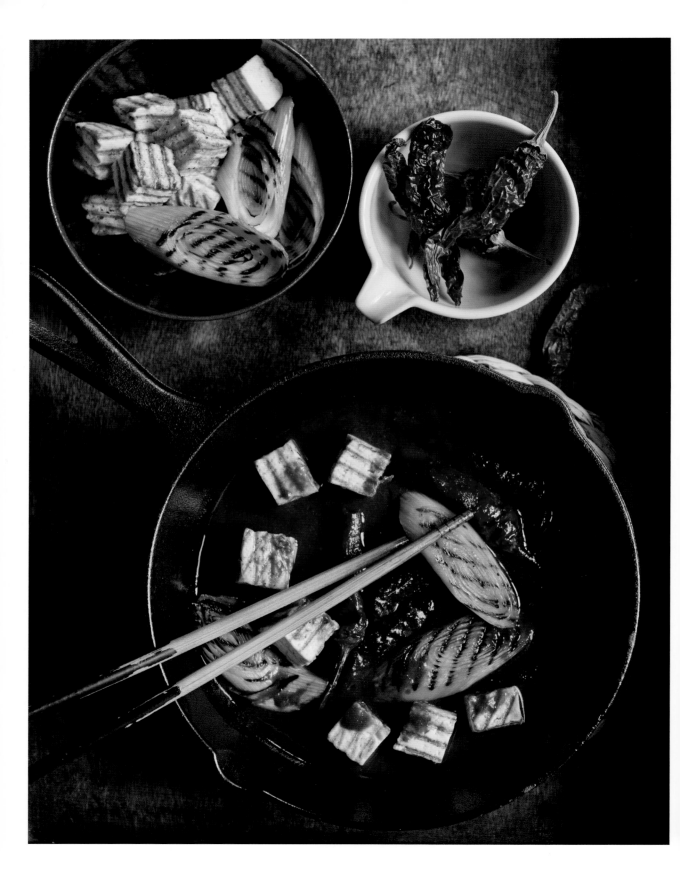

CHILI TOFU

You can eat this as a side dish or as a snack. I like to eat it with rice, but westerners may find it a bit dry that way.

Serves 2

— **12 oz [350 g] firm tofu, cut into ¾ in [2 cm] cubes**
— **½ leek, cut into ⅜ in [1 cm] slices**
— **6 dried red chiles**

For the sauce
— **2 Tbsp white miso**
— **2 Tbsp sake or vodka**
— **1 Tbsp soy sauce**
— **1 tsp superfine sugar**
— **2 Tbsp balsamic vinegar**

Preheat the broiler to its highest setting, or heat a griddle pan if you want griddle marks. Pat the tofu with paper towels to get rid of any water, then broil it and the leek on both sides for 3 minutes each, until brown. At the same time, broil the dried chiles for 3 minutes. This should be just enough to bring their flavors out, but don't blacken or scorch them. You can griddle all the components instead, if you prefer.

Meanwhile, make the sauce. Mix the miso with the sake and place into a small saucepan. Add the chiles and cook for a few minutes until flavored.

Add the soy sauce, sugar, and 3 Tbsp [50 ml] water and bring to a simmer. Once it's boiling, reduce the heat to low and add the balsamic vinegar.

Add the tofu and leek and cook over low heat for 15 to 20 minutes until the liquid has been absorbed.

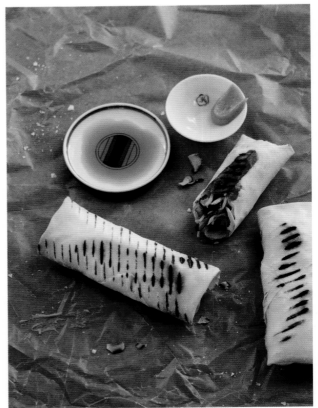

MUSTARD CHICKEN

A more westernized dish, even though my Japanese dad invented it! It's great for summer eating.

Serves 2

— 10½ oz [300 g] skin-on boneless chicken thighs, cut into ¾ in [2 cm] strips
— Sprinkling of sake or vodka
— ½ onion, grated
— Pinch of sea salt and freshly ground black pepper
— Shredded lettuce
— Finely sliced onions

For the marinade
— ½ tsp grated garlic
— 1 tsp soy sauce
— 2 tsp brown sugar
— 1 Tbsp French mustard
— ½ Tbsp English mustard

Lay the chicken on a tray and sprinkle with sake. Stir in the onion and some seasoning. Set aside to marinate for 10 minutes. Preheat the broiler to its highest setting.

Transfer the chicken to a grill pan or baking sheet and broil both sides for 4 to 5 minutes. Once it is nice and brown, put it in a bowl with the marinade ingredients and mix well.

Return the chicken to the pan and broil for another few minutes.

Serve with shredded lettuce and finely sliced onions.

BROILED SPRING ROLLS

Instead of frying spring rolls in the usual manner, these broiled or grilled versions are low in oil and (of course) calories, but are nevertheless wonderfully crisp.

Makes 6 to 7

— 12 oz [350 g] pork, cut into wafer-thin slices
— 1 Tbsp sake or vodka
— 1 tsp soy sauce
— 3½ oz [100 g] shiitake mushrooms, finely sliced
— Scant ½ cup [50 g] bamboo shoots (canned is fine), finely sliced
— 2 scallions, cut into 4 in [10 cm] strips
— 2 in [1 thumb] ginger root, finely sliced
— Handful of cilantro leaves and stalks
— 1 tsp sesame oil
— 1 Tbsp cornstarch
— 6 to 7 spring roll sheets

Mix the pork with the sake and soy sauce, cover, and leave to marinate for 20 minutes.

Put the pork, mushrooms, bamboo shoots, scallions, ginger, coriander, and sesame oil in a bowl and mix well with your hands.

Mix the cornstarch with enough water to make a smooth paste (you will be using it as a "glue").

Place a spring roll sheet on a work surface. Put a handful of the pork mixture in the center of the sheet.

Fold over two opposite corners (left and right) of the spring roll sheet just to cover the ends of the filling, then roll from the bottom to the top of the sheet, brushing the cornstarch mixture around the edges to seal it well. Repeat to use up all the filling and spring roll sheets.

Put the rolls on a pan, sealed sides down. Preheat the broiler to a medium setting, or heat a griddle pan. Broil or griddle for 10 minutes, turning, until nicely bronzed.

MAKI'S COD MISO

This has a nice soft and melting texture and quite
a strong miso flavor. With the Shoku-Iku style of
eating, a few dishes should be arranged together,
so you might eat this fish with miso soup with tofu
and seaweed, pickles, or rice, as in the photo. Let
the power of five (see pages 7 to 15) inform your
choices: you should aim for a good mixture of food
groups, textures, colors, and cooking methods.

Serves 4

For the fish
— **4 4-oz [120 g] fillets of cod**
  (fresh is better than frozen for this)
— **Pinch of sea salt**
— **3 Tbsp sake or vodka**
— **⅓ cup [40 g] grated daikon**

For the paste
— **3 Tbsp mirin**
— **4 Tbsp sake or vodka**
— **1 heaping cup [300 g] white miso**

Lay the cod on a tray and sprinkle with the sea salt
and sake. Set aside for 10 minutes.

Mix all the ingredients for the paste.

Smooth half the paste onto a small pan which can fit
all the cod in a single layer. Place the cod on top and
coat with the rest of the paste, covering the fish
completely. Seal with plastic wrap and leave in the
fridge overnight.

Next day, scrape any excess paste from the cod.
Preheat the broiler to a medium setting. Broil the cod
for 10 minutes until lightly brown. Cover with foil
and leave it for another 3 minutes.

Serve with the daikon.

MAKI'S MISO PORK

I usually marinate this before I go to bed and cook the next day. Serve with steamed broccoli and rice.

Serves 2 to 3

— 2 pork fillets, 14 to 18 oz [400 to 500 g], sliced into ¼ in [5 mm] slices
— 2 Tbsp white miso
— 1 Tbsp sake or white wine
— 1 tsp honey
— 1 tsp soy sauce
— 1 tsp mirin
— 2 tsp sesame oil
— 1 tsp grated garlic
— 1 orange, peeled and sliced
— 2 handfuls of salad leaves

Put the pork in a plastic food bag and add all the other ingredients except the orange and salad leaves. Seal the bag, while pushing out all the air you can, then massage it for one minute to really help the marinade to penetrate the meat. Leave the bag in the fridge overnight.

Preheat the broiler to its highest setting, or heat a griddle pan. Lightly broil or griddle both sides of the pork until it is dark brown, then serve with the orange slices and salad leaves.

MAKI'S RICE CRACKERS

These are meant as a between-meal snack
or for lunch boxes.

Makes 2

— 1 to 1¼ cups [120 to 150 g] cooked Japanese
  glutinous rice (see page 110), warm or cold
— ½ tsp sesame oil
— 1 Tbsp mirin
— 1 Tbsp soy sauce

Lay a 12 in [30 cm] long sheet of wax paper on
a worktop and put half the rice in the middle. Fold
the paper in half and flatten the pile of rice until it
is ¼ in [5 mm] thick. Repeat with the other half of
the rice.

Heat a frying pan over medium heat with the
sesame oil.

Fry the rice patties on both sides for a total of 2
minutes. Separately, mix together the mirin and soy
sauces. Brush the rice patties with the sauce and
turn, repeating this brushing and turning 3 to 4
times until brown.

Serve immediately, or cover the pan and reheat the
crackers when required.

SWEET POTATO DREAM

You can put carrots in this as well if you want to hide
them! It's beautifully sweet and they will slip down
unnoticed. This is a very authentic dessert or snack,
great to eat instead of any cakes containing wheat
or flour. Another one good for lunch boxes.

Serves 4/Makes 10 to 12

— 1 large sweet potato, about 10 oz [300 g],
  peeled and cut into ⅜ in [1 cm] cubes
— 2½ Tbsp brown sugar
— 2 tsp honey
— 1 egg yolk, lightly beaten

Place the sweet potato in a microwaveable pan and
cover with plastic wrap. Microwave for 6 minutes.

Once the potato is soft, add the sugar and mash well.
Add the honey and stir until smooth.

Hold a 8 in [20 cm] wide piece of plastic wrap in your
hand and place 2 Tbsp of potato mix in the center.
Close your hand, shaping it into an oval. Repeat with
the remainder of the mix.

Preheat the broiler to its highest setting. Unwrap the
potato mix "eggs" and brush the beaten egg yolk all
over. Transfer to a grill pan and broil for 3 minutes,
turning, or until brown on all sides.

Serve warm or cold.

NO-COOK

"Turn off your oven and discover
a whole new way to prepare food."

Japanese cuisine is famous for raw fish and it's hardly surprising that many of my recipes require absolutely no heat or cooking. There are some previously cooked foods in this chapter —such as shrimp and tofu—but not many. And you don't have to cook them yourself. For me, the benefits of no-cooking are plentiful.

First and foremost, raw foods sum up the Shoku-Iku ethos of goodness, nutrition, and conscious eating, as there is no surer way to preserve a food's integrity and goodness. I also find that, when eating raw foods, it's natural that you would select variety. For instance, my salads are made from numerous vegetables and herbs and not just from green leaves. This chapter also illustrates how raw foods can be made extra tasty simply with the addition of other raw ingredients, which have been pickled instead of cooked to intensify their flavors.

Raw foods contain far higher levels of nutrients than cooked foods; some nutritionists believe up to one-third more. Without the effects of cooking, foods also retain far higher levels of fiber. Raw food exercises our gums and jaws as we chew it, boosts the immune system, and brightens our skin, especially if you include seeds and nuts in the mix.

Fresh and raw food also looks so beautiful. The colors of natural uncooked foods are so vibrant and appealing. Once you get into the habit of incorporating raw foods into your daily diet, a plate of cooked food can look dull beside them. Because raw food retains its natural moisture content, it helps you to feel full but not as though you have overeaten. Once you start consciously mixing raw dishes into your daily meals, you won't look back.

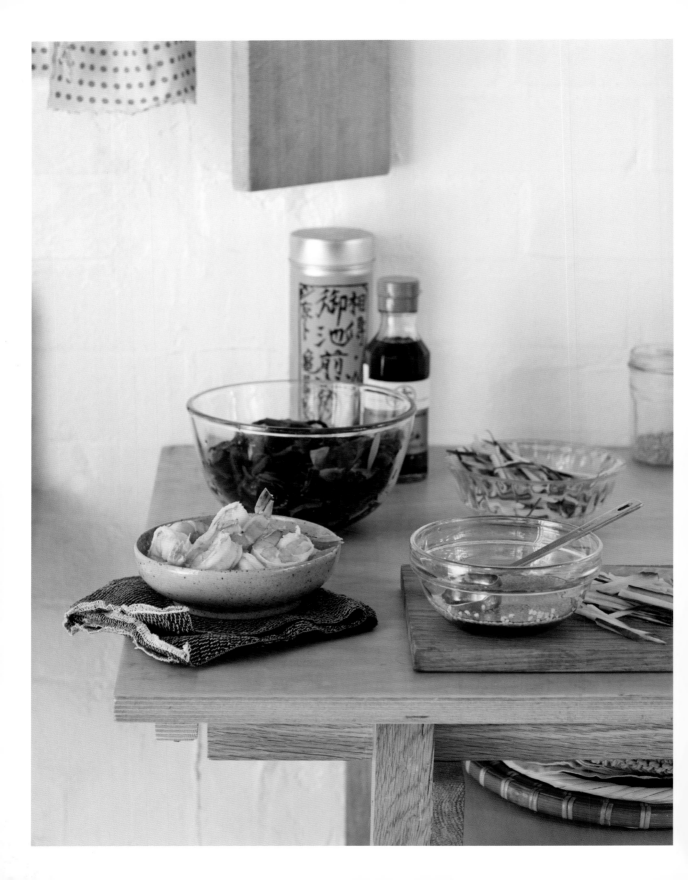

VINEGARED SHRIMP SALAD

This is a lovely side dish, with piquant, satisfying
flavors. The dried seaweed you need here is the
shredded type.

Serves 2 to 3

— **2 cups [40 g] dried seaweed**
— **1 cucumber, sliced into julienne**
— **6 cooked, peeled shrimp, deveined
  if necessary**

For the dressing
— **⅓ tsp sea salt**
— **2 Tbsp rice vinegar**
— **2 Tbsp superfine sugar or honey**
— **1 tsp white sesame seeds**
— **1 tsp soy sauce**

Soak the seaweed in a bowl in 4½ cups [1 L] water
for 20 minutes. Drain and squeeze to make sure
you remove all the water.

Meanwhile, put the salt, vinegar, and sugar in a
separate bowl and mix until the sugar dissolves.
Add the sesame seeds and mix well.

Add the seaweed, cucumber, and shrimp to the
sauce and mix well. Cover and leave in the fridge
for 30 minutes. Serve, stirring in the soy sauce.

JAPANESE PICKLES

This side dish can be eaten with anything, or even
just with plain rice as a palate enlivener.

Makes 5 to 6 small servings

— **5 Napa cabbage leaves, cut into ⅜ in [1 cm]
    slices**
— **1 whole cucumber, cut into ⅜ in [1 cm] slices**
— **2 white turnips, cut into ⅜ in [1 cm] slices,
    or 6 to 8 small turnips, quartered**
— **1 onion, cut into ¼ in [5 mm] slices**

For the sauce
— **½ tsp white sesame seeds, crushed**
    (see page 19), **plus 1 tsp whole white
    sesame seeds**
— **2 tsp rice vinegar**
— **2 tsp soy sauce**
— **2 tsp sesame oil**

Pour all the ingredients for the sauce, except the
whole sesame seeds, into a plastic food bag and add
all the vegetables. Seal well and put it in the fridge
for 1 hour.

Drain all the liquid and serve in a small bowl with
the white sesame seeds sprinkled on top.

This will keep, covered, in the fridge for 7 days.
If it throws off a lot of liquid in that time, simply drain
it off before using.

ICED TOMATO

These make a really refreshing mouthful and are perfect for summer; I can eat two or three at a time! They are really good with barbecued food.

Makes 4

— **4 medium tomatoes**

For the sauce
— **2 Tbsp soy sauce**
— **1 Tbsp mirin**
— **1 tsp superfine sugar**
— **1 tsp sea salt**
— **2¼ cups [800 ml] Basic dashi** (see page 18)

For the topping
— **5 oba leaves, or cilantro leaves, shredded**
— **½ shallot, finely sliced**
— **1 in [½ thumb] ginger root, grated**

Peel the tomatoes (see page 53). Mix together all the ingredients for the sauce.

Coat the whole tomatoes with the sauce in a large bowl, then seal it with plastic wrap. Chill in the fridge for 1 day.

Serve in a small bowl and sprinkle the oba, shallot, and ginger on top.

SPINACH SALAD

Although you might think of this as a side dish or a light lunch, my mom actually eats it every morning at breakfast. She always wants to have greens at breakfast, to get as many in as she can. Shoku-Iku!

Serves 2 as a side dish

— **Handful of baby spinach**
— **5 lettuce leaves, cut into ¾ in [2 cm] strips**

For the dressing
— **1 Tbsp honey**
— **2 Tbsp Noodle soup stock** (see page 18)
— **1 Tbsp white sesame seeds, crushed** (see page 19)
— **2 Tbsp sesame oil**
— **1 sheet of dried nori, crumbled**

Mix together all the ingredients for the dressing.

Put the spinach and lettuce in a bowl and add the dressing. Stir together and serve.

BELGIAN ENDIVE WITH COD ROE SALAD

You could serve this as a canapé or a very elegant starter. I first made it for a friend's wedding and it was a great success. Obviously scale up the quantities to make more.

Makes 5

— 2 oz [50 g] smoked cod roe (or anchovy),
  very finely sliced
— 1 medium stalk [40 g] celery, finely sliced
— 5 Belgian endive leaves
— 1 tsp canola oil

Mix the cod roe and celery in a bowl.

Place spoonfuls of the cod roe mixture on Belgian endive leaves and sprinkle with canola oil.

HONEY TOMATO WITH TOFU

Image on page 96

This is a kind of salad, and meant as a side dish. I prefer it with silken tofu, but it is also good with the firm kind, if you like. It is great with Hot steamed chicken and Mustard chicken (see pages 60 and 79).

Serves 3 to 4

— 1 large tomato, seeded and cut into ⅜ in
  [1 cm] pieces (see page 53), or leave it
  chunky, if you prefer
— 1 large shallot, minced
— 12 oz [350 g] silken or firm tofu, cut into
  3-in-by-⅜-in [3-cm-by-1-cm] batons, or cubes
— a few small cilantro leaves

For the dressing
— 1 Tbsp honey
— 1 Tbsp balsamic vinegar
— 1 Tbsp soy sauce

Put the tomato and shallot into a small bowl. Mix all the ingredients for the dressing and add to the bowl. Mix well and place in the fridge for 30 minutes.

Lay the tofu on a plate and place the tomato and shallots on top. Dress with the cilantro leaves.

KALE SALAD

Image on page 97

You can eat this warm, though it is more usually
served cold. Kale has quite a strong flavor,
so you don't need a lot.

Serves 3 to 4 as a side dish

— **8 kale leaves, coarse ribs removed, cut into
  1½ in [4 cm] strips**
— **1 Tbsp white sesame seeds, crushed**
  (see page 19)
— **1 Tbsp light soy sauce**
— **2 Tbsp sesame oil**

Put the kale in a pan and add ¼ cup [50 ml] water.
Cover and simmer for 3 to 5 minutes, or until tender.
Squeeze the liquid from the kale.

Place the kale in a serving bowl and add all the other
ingredients. Mix well and serve with meat dishes.

OKRA WITH CANNED TUNA

This is a kind of fusion dish, with western and
Japanese influences.

Serves 2 as a side dish

— **10 okra fingers, blanched for 2 minutes**
  (see page 75)
— **⅔ cup [160 g] canned tuna in spring water,
  drained**

For the sauce
— **1 tsp lemon juice**
— **2 tsp French mustard**
— **½ tsp light soy sauce**

Cut each okra finger into pieces.

Put the tuna in a bowl. In a separate bowl,
mix together all the ingredients for the sauce.

Mix the tuna and sauce with the okra, turning to coat,
then serve immediately.

FIVE SENSES SUSHI

"People shouldn't be afraid of creating sushi. Don't worry about being too authentic; just enjoy the process. Here are some imaginative ways to get you started. Great tasting and great fun, too."

Sushi for me, with all its accompanying pastes and pickles, is one of the tastiest of foods and its soaring popularity in the West is testament to this.

If you have never thought about creating your own sushi, then start thinking! You only need some bamboo rolling mats, sushi or Japanese rice, and a good bottle of rice vinegar. I find most people's resistance to making sushi at home comes from the mistaken idea that it will be too tricky to make. In fact it couldn't be simpler, and once you have perfected cooking good Japanese rice, it is barely more complicated than making a sandwich. I have taught thousands (literally) of people to make sushi and I always tell them what I will tell you now: as long as you enjoy the taste, it doesn't matter if at first it doesn't look perfectly neat. That comes with practice.

Sushi is a soothing meal, refreshing during hotter months, but also perfect as a meal following any over-indulgence as it doesn't sit heavily on the stomach. If you eat it for lunch, you won't feel weighed down as you tackle the afternoon's work.

The effect of eating sushi on your health and your senses is well documented: the omega-3 rich fish, the iron-boosting seaweed wrapper, and the nonfat energy from rice. Even the pickled ginger has been found to aid digestion, while wasabi has been identified as having tooth-protective qualities as well as ensuring fresh breath.

The beauty and colors of sushi—as well as its nourishing and sense-stimulating qualities—make it the epitome of Shoku-Iku foods.

AVOCADO AND PEAR QUINOA POWER SUSHI

I always put plastic wrap around my sushi rolling mats before using, as this prevents the rice (or quinoa, in this case) from sticking at all. For a step-by-step guide to how to roll sushi, see page 21.

Serves 2 to 3

— **Scant 1¼ cups [200 g] quinoa**
— **3 Tbsp puréed or mashed mango**
  (mashed with a fork)
— **1 tsp white wine vinegar**
— **1 tsp lemon juice**
— **Pinch of sea salt**
— **1 medium pear**
— **4 to 5 full sheets of dried nori seaweed**
— **1 avocado, finely sliced**

Place the quinoa into a sieve and rinse well under cold water. Pour the rinsed quinoa into a saucepan, add 1⅔ cups [400 ml] water and cook over medium heat.

Bring to a boil, then reduce the heat to a simmer. Cook for about 13 minutes until soft, stirring frequently. Drain well to remove any excess water.

Put the cooked quinoa in a bowl and let it cool to lukewarm for few minutes.

Add the mango purée, vinegar, lemon juice, and sea salt to the quinoa while still warm and mix well. Transfer to a , spreading the quinoa thinly, and allow it to cool completely.

Meanwhile, preheat the broiler. Finely slice the pear and broil the slices for 2 or 3 minutes on each side.

Place a nori sheet on a sushi rolling mat, long side towards you and rough side up, shiny side down. Spread ¼ to ⅕ (depending on whether you are making 4 or 5 rolls) of the quinoa mix from the bottom to ⅔ of the way up the sheet.

Place 4 slices of avocado and 3 slices of lightly broiled pear along the middle of the quinoa. Roll the nori tightly up to the end. Leave it to sit for two to three minutes to allow the seaweed to soften.

Repeat to use up all the nori sheets, rice and filling.

Cut each roll into 6 pieces, then serve.

BROWN SUSHI RICE

I always cook brown rice in a pressure cooker, as I find it most convenient that way. It is hard to cook smaller quantities than this, so if you find you have too much for a recipe, freeze the rest. Never refrigerate it, as that will spoil the texture.

Makes enough for 2 to 3

— Scant 2¼ cups [400 g] brown sushi rice
— 2¼ cups [500 ml] cold water
— Scant ½ cup [100 ml] sushi vinegar

Rinse the rice quickly under cold water, then drain. Place the rice and measured water into a pressure cooker. Wait until it comes to a boil, then reduce the heat to low and cook for about 20 minutes.

Remove the lid quickly so the moisture doesn't drip down on onto the rice.

Wait until the pressure cooker cools down, then transfer the hot rice to a shallow bowl.

Add the sushi vinegar and mix well. Spread it out thinly on a tray and let it cool to lukewarm.

BROWN SHIITAKE AND PUMPKIN SUSHI

Always season sushi rice with vinegar while it is still hot, so it soaks up all the flavors (see left). I designed this recipe to be rolled so the rice ends up on the outside, like a California roll, but you can roll it the more conventional way as well, as we did for the photo. For a step-by-step guide to how to roll both types, see page 21.

Serves 2 to 3

— 10 shiitake mushrooms, stems removed, finely sliced
— ¼ pumpkin, finely sliced
— Sea salt
— 1 lb [450 g] Brown sushi rice, cooked and seasoned with sushi vinegar, lukewarm (see left)
— 3 half sheets of dried nori seaweed.
— handful of spinach leaves

Preheat the broiler to its highest setting, or heat a griddle pan. Grill the mushrooms and pumpkin, both sprinkled with sea salt, on both sides, until cooked.

Take about ⅓ of the rice and spread all over the rough side of a half sheet of nori on a rolling mat.

Flip the sheet upside down so the seaweed is on the top, facing you. The roll should still be on the mat.

Place ⅓ of the spinach, pumpkin, and mushrooms in a row across the seaweed.

Roll, leaving the brown rice on the outside. Repeat with the other half sheets of nori and the remaining rice and filling.

Cut each roll into 6 pieces, then serve.

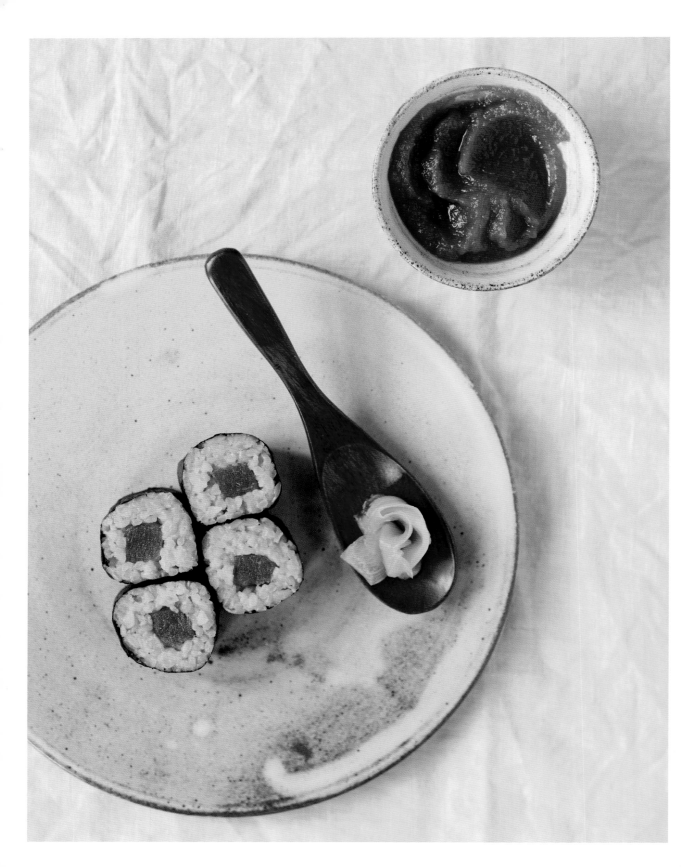

BROWN RICE TUNA SUSHI
WITH SWEET-HOT SAUCE

The sauce here is sweet and spicy and very addictive.
A hugely satisfying dish. Again, you can choose to roll
this in the conventional manner or as a California roll,
as you prefer. For a step-by-step guide to how to roll
both types, see page 21.

Serves 2 to 3

For the sauce
— **1 apple, peeled, cored, and chopped**
— **1 Tbsp honey**
— **1 Tbsp mirin**
— **1 Tbsp wasabi powder**
— **1 Tbsp light soy sauce**

For the sushi
— **Scant ½ cup [100 ml] dry sake or vodka**
— **3½ oz [100 g] sushi-grade tuna, sliced
   into batons**
— **1 lb [450 g] Brown sushi rice, cooked
   and seasoned with sushi vinegar, lukewarm**
   (see page 104)
— **3 half sheets of dried nori seaweed**

Put the apple, honey and mirin in a saucepan and
cook for 15 to 20 minutes over medium heat until the
apple is soft. Put the apple mix in a blender and add
the wasabi and soy sauce. Blend until smooth.

Pour the sake into a bowl and add the tuna. Leave
to soak for 20 to 30 minutes.

Take about ⅓ of the rice and spread all over the rough
side of a half sheet of nori on a rolling mat.

Flip the sheet upside down so the seaweed is on the
top, facing you. It should still be on the mat.

Place ⅓ of the marinated tuna in a row across the
seaweed. Then roll, leaving the brown rice on the
outside. Repeat with the other half sheets of nori and
the remaining rice and filling.

Cut each roll into 6 pieces, then serve, with the sauce
on top or on the side.

WHITE SUSHI RICE

This may make more than you need for the recipes here, but it freezes really well in smaller portions once cooked. Never put cooked sushi rice in the fridge, as that will ruin its yielding texture.

Makes enough for 5 to 6

— 2½ cups [600 ml] white sushi rice
  (best measured in a measuring cup)
— 2 ¾ cups [660 ml] cold water
— ½ cup [120 ml] sushi vinegar

Wash the rice thoroughly, then leave it to dry for at least 30 minutes in a sieve.

 a large pan with a tight-fitting lid. I find a casserole dish better for cooking this rice than a regular saucepan.

Measure the water and put it in the pan. Pour in the rice. Place over medium heat, cover, and leave for 10 to 13 minutes, until it comes to a boil (listen for the bubbles; do not remove the lid).

When the water has come to a boil, reduce the heat to its lowest setting for 30 seconds, then turn the heat off. Leave it for 15 minutes with the lid on.

Place the hot rice in a shallow bowl, add the sushi vinegar and mix well. Spread the rice thinly on a tray and let it cool to lukewarm.

SESAME SEED SALMON SUSHI

By blending the sesame seeds, your body can access all the good nutrition inside them. For a step-by-step guide to how to roll sushi, see page 21.

Serves 2 to 3

— 3½ Tbsp [30 g] white sesame seeds
— 3½ Tbsp [30 g] black sesame seeds
— Heaping 1½ cups [300 g] White sushi rice,
  cooked and seasoned with sushi vinegar,
  lukewarm (see left)
— 1 tsp sesame oil
— Pinch of sea salt
— 5 oz [150 g] sushi-grade salmon fillet,
  finely sliced
— 2 half sheets of dried nori seaweed
— 1 cucumber, cut into julienne

Mix ⅔ [20 g] of both types of sesame seeds in a bowl. Put the remainder in a blender and blitz into a powder. Add this sesame powder to the cooked rice and mix well. Then add the whole sesame seeds to the rice and stir them in, too.

Massage the sesame oil and sea salt onto the salmon and leave for five minutes.

Take about ½ of the rice mix and spread it all over the rough side of a half sheet of nori on a rolling mat.

Flip the sheet upside down so the seaweed is on the top, facing you. It should still be on the mat.

Place ½ of the marinated salmon and cucumber in a row across the seaweed.

Roll, leaving the white rice on the outside. Repeat with the other half nori sheet, rice and filling.

Cut each roll into 6 pieces, then serve.

SUSHI CUP CAKES

Image on page 108

This is a cute idea and everyone loves them.

Makes 10

— **1 oz [30 g] sushi-grade or smoked salmon, finely sliced** (at least 10 pieces)
— **1 oz [30 g] sushi-grade sea bream or sea bass, finely sliced** (at least 10 pieces)
— **1 oz [30 g] sushi-grade tuna steak, finely sliced** (at least 10 pieces)
— **2 slices of prosciutto, finely sliced lengthwise** (at least 10 pieces)
— **2⅛ cups [400 g] White sushi rice, cooked and seasoned with sushi vinegar** (see page 110), **lukewarm**
— **1¼ in [3 cm] block of hard cheese, finely cubed**
— **2 oba leaves, or cilantro leaves, minced**
— **1 heaping Tbsp [10 g] white sesame seeds**

Cut out 10 x 4-by-6-in [10-by-15-cm] squares of plastic wrap. Place a plastic wrap square in your hand. Put one slice each of salmon, sea bream, tuna, and prosciutto in the middle of the plastic wrap.

Put $^1/_{10}$ [40 g] of rice on top of the fish and prosciutto. Close your hand and twist the plastic wrap edges to make a ball. Repeat to make 10 balls. Unwrap from the plastic wrap.

Place each of the balls in a paper cupcake case. Sprinkle with the cheese, oba leaves, and sesame seeds to decorate.

BOUQUET OF FLOWERS TEMAKI

Image on page 109

The idea of this is that the filling ingredients should spill out of the top of the sushi cones.

Serves 3 to 4

— **7 half sheets of dried nori seaweed**
— **2¼ cups [420 g] White sushi rice, cooked and seasoned with sushi vinegar, lukewarm** (see page 110)
— **7 oba leaves, or cilantro leaves, minced**
— **Handful of salad leaves**
— **3½ oz [100 g] sushi-grade or smoked salmon, finely sliced**
— **3½ oz [100 g] sushi-grade tuna, finely sliced**
— **3½ oz [100 g] sushi-grade sea bream or sea bass, finely sliced**
— **½ cucumber, finely sliced**
— **1 avocado, finely sliced**
— **7 cooked shrimp, peeled**

Cut 7 sheets of wax paper the same size as the sheets of nori.

Place one of the wax paper sheets in your hand and place one half sheet of nori on top, rough side facing you.

Place $^1/_7$ [60 g] of rice onto the left-hand side of the sheet of nori, spreading it evenly.

Add $^1/_7$ of the other ingredients across the rice, in a line from top right to bottom left.

Use your thumb to push the bottom corner of nori across to the middle. Then fold the rest of the seaweed around to form a cone shape.

Repeat to make seven of these rolls. Place in a shallow bowl or vase to look like bouquets.

SALMON, ROE, AND AVOCADO SUSHI CAKE

If you are at all nervous about rolling sheets of dried seaweed, this is the recipe for you. It's very easy. Obviously just scale the recipe up to make more "cakes." You will need a round metal cooking ring 3¼ in [8 cm] wide and 2¾ in [7 cm] high.

Makes 1 portion

— Scant ½ cup [80 g] White sushi rice, cooked and seasoned with sushi vinegar, lukewarm (see page 110)
— 1 avocado, skinned and cut into ⅜ in [1 cm] pieces
— 2 oz [50 g] sushi-grade or smoked salmon, chopped into small pieces
— 1 oz [25 g] salmon roe

Place the cooking ring onto a serving plate. Press ½ of the cooked rice evenly in a layer in the ring.

Top with an even layer of avocado chunks, then the salmon pieces.

Press in a second layer of rice. Add the roe on top, nice and evenly, then gently pull the ring away.

FLOWER CAKE

This is an impressive and beautiful thing, sure to wow your guests. To construct it, use a 4¾ in [12 cm] tart ring. If you line it with plastic wrap, you will find it easier to remove the cake without trouble.

Serves 3 to 4

For the egg ribbons
— 1 Tbsp mirin or superfine sugar
— ½ tsp sea salt
— 3 eggs, lightly beaten

For the cake
— 2 scant cups [360 g] White sushi rice, cooked and seasoned with sushi vinegar, lukewarm (see page 110)
— 2 heaping Tbsp [20 g] white sesame seeds
— 1 avocado, finely sliced
— 3½ oz [100 g] sushi-grade tuna steak, cut into ⅜ in [1 cm] cubes
— 4 in [10 cm] chunk of cucumber, finely sliced into discs
— 2 oz [50 g] sushi-grade salmon steak, cut into ⅜ in [1 cm] cubes
— 5 oz [150 g] salmon roe
— beansprouts, or sprigs of cilantro, to serve

Start with the egg ribbons. Add the mirin or sugar and salt to the egg. Cook it in a shallow sauté pan to make a thin omelet. When it has cooled down, roll it into a tube and slice it finely into shreds.

Now for the cake. Use a springform pan or a 4¾ in [12 cm] tart ring lined with plastic wrap. Mix the cooked rice with the white sesame seeds and use this mixture to line the bottom of the pan.

Gently lay the egg ribbons along the outer edge of the rice. Make a concentric circle, next to the egg but within it, of the avocado slices.

Layer cubes of tuna in a circle next to the avocado. Then make a circle of cucumber discs next to the tuna. As you work inwards, place the salmon chunks toward the center. In the very center place your salmon roe.

Garnish with beansprouts or sprigs of coriander and serve immediately.

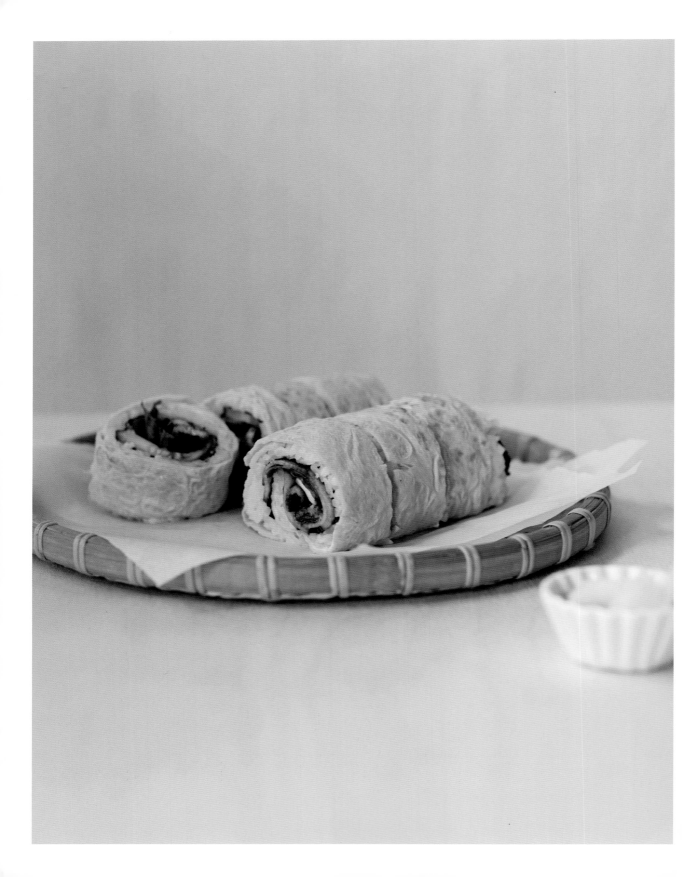

EGG AND EEL SUSHI ROLL

There are strong flavors here, but the rich, oily eel is so very good for you and so utterly delicious. For a step-by-step guide to how to roll sushi, see page 21.

Serves 2 to 3

— **5 shiitake mushrooms, stems removed, finely sliced**
— **Sea salt**
— **1 full sheet of dried nori seaweed**
— **Heaping 1½ cups [300 g] White sushi rice, cooked and seasoned with sushi vinegar, lukewarm** (see page 110)
— **3 x 4-in [10-cm] lengths of cucumber, finely sliced into discs**
— **7 oz [200 g] roasted eel, sliced into ¾ in [2 cm] pieces**
— **Handful of baby spinach, washed**
— **½ tsp cornstarch**
— **1 tsp dashi flakes**
— **3 eggs, lightly beaten**

Preheat the broiler. Broil the mushrooms, sprinkled with sea salt, on both sides, until cooked.

Place the nori sheet, rough side up, on a flat surface. Spread the rice evenly all over the nori.

Flip the sheet upside down so the seaweed is on the top, facing you.

Place the cucumber discs up the nori from the bottom, leaving the top ⅓ of the nori clear.

Place the roasted eel across the middle of the cucumber. Lay shiitake mushroom slices over the eel, then the spinach over the mushrooms. Put a sushi rolling mat over everything and press it gently to ensure it is held together well.

Add the cornstarch, dashi flakes, and a pinch more sea salt to the beaten eggs. Make a thin omelet with this in a sauté pan; it should be about 1½ times bigger than the nori sheet.

Place the egg onto the rolling mat. Place your sushi roll on top. Roll the omelet up with the sushi roll. Leave it whole for a short while, to settle, then cut into six pieces to serve.

FIVE SENSES SUPER-TASTY SALMON SUSHI

As usual, simply scale up the amounts here to feed more people. You can use either tobanjan or the Korean spicy paste gochujang; both can be bought from Asian food stores or online. For a step-by-step guide to how to roll sushi, see page 21.

Serves 1

— **3½ oz [100 g] sushi-grade salmon**
— **1 half sheet of dried nori seaweed**
— **Heaping ¾ cup [150 g] White sushi rice, cooked and seasoned with sushi vinegar, lukewarm** (see page 110)
— **4 in [10 cm] cucumber, finely sliced**
— **½ avocado, finely sliced**
— **1 scallion, minced**

For the marinade
— **1 Tbsp sesame oil**
— **1 tsp tobanjan or gochujang**
— **1 Tbsp sake or vodka**
— **Pinch of sea salt**

Grill the salmon lightly on a griddle pan just so the surface is seared, about 1 minute on each side, then slice very finely.

Mix together all the ingredients for the marinade and use to coat the salmon slices in a small bowl. Leave to marinate for 5 minutes.

Place the nori, rough side up, onto a sushi rolling mat. Spread the rice evenly all over.

Flip the sheet upside down so the seaweed is on the top, facing you. It should still be on the mat. Add the cucumber and avocado in the center of the sheet. Roll it all the way up.

Wrap the salmon around the rice roll. Put the sushi rolling mat on top of the salmon and squeeze the roll gently to ensure it is held together well. Cut into 6 or 8 pieces.

Sprinkle with the scallion and serve.

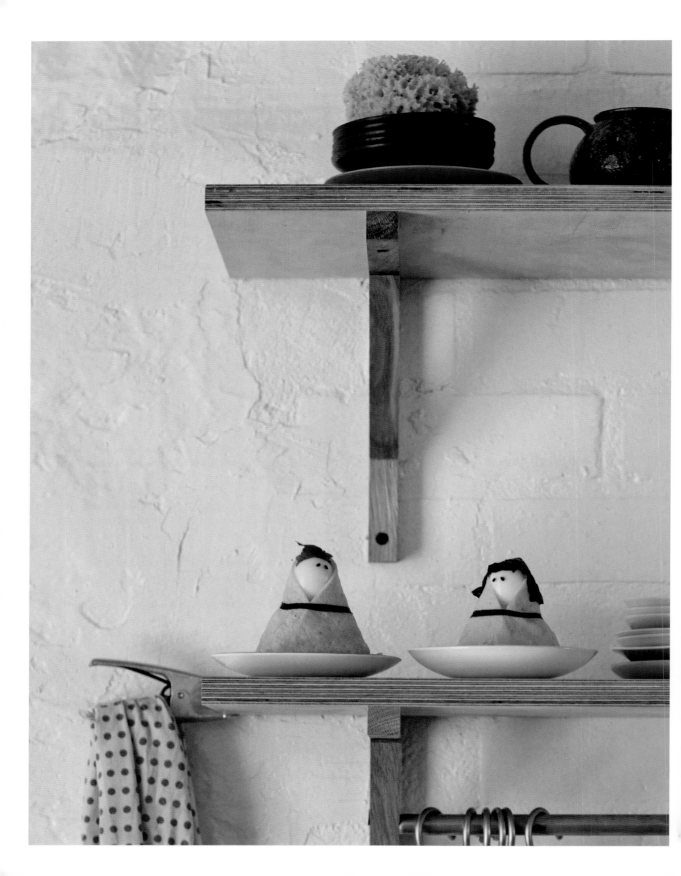

WASABI CREAM CHEESE SUSHI

Red meat and cream cheese aren't ingredients you would usually find in sushi; this is a good way to introduce sushi to more nervous western palates. Scale the recipe up to make more. For a step-by-step guide to how to roll sushi, see page 21.

Serves 1

— 1 oz [30 g] lamb steak, finely sliced
— Heaping ¾ cup [150 g] White sushi rice, cooked and seasoned with sushi vinegar, lukewarm (see page 110)
— 1 half sheet of dried nori seaweed
— 1 heaping Tbsp [10 g] mixed white and black sesame seeds
— 2 Tbsp [30 g] cream cheese
— 1 Tbsp wasabi
— Pinch of freshly ground black pepper
— 7 chives
— Small handful of arugula salad leaves

Broil the slices of lamb for 5 minutes, turning once.

Spread the sushi rice onto the rough side of the nori, on a rolling mat. Sprinkle the sesame seeds evenly on top of the rice.

Flip the sheet upside down so the seaweed is on the top, facing you. It should still be on the mat. Mix the cream cheese with the wasabi and black pepper, then spread it in the center of the seaweed.

Place the chives, lamb, and arugula on top of the cream cheese and roll.

Cut the roll into 6 pieces, then serve.

DOLL CAKES

Go on, just try to resist these. They are amazingly cute and appeal to the palates of children.

Makes 2 dolls

— 2 quail eggs
— 2 eggs, lightly beaten
— Heaping 1½ cups [300 g] White sushi rice, cooked and seasoned with sushi vinegar, lukewarm (see page 110)
— 1 full sheet of dried nori seaweed
— 4 black sesame seeds (for eyes)

Hard-boil the quail eggs in boiling water for 2½ to 3 minutes, then drain. Peel them carefully. They need to stay as unblemished as possible, as these are the dolls' heads.

Heat a 10 in [25 cm] frying pan and cook the beaten eggs to make a thin omelet.

Mold two cones with the rice. Cut the omelet in half to make 2 half moon shapes. Wrap each half around the rice cone to create a cloak/kimono.

Cut two strips of nori ⅜ in [1 cm] wide and 8 in [20 cm] long and wrap one around each cloak/kimono like a belt. Seal with water. Using a toothpick, join a quail's egg to the top of each rice cone body.

Gently push two sesame seeds into each egg to form eyes. Use tiny strips of nori to create hair shapes on top of each egg.

Depending how artistic you are feeling, you can add extra adornments!

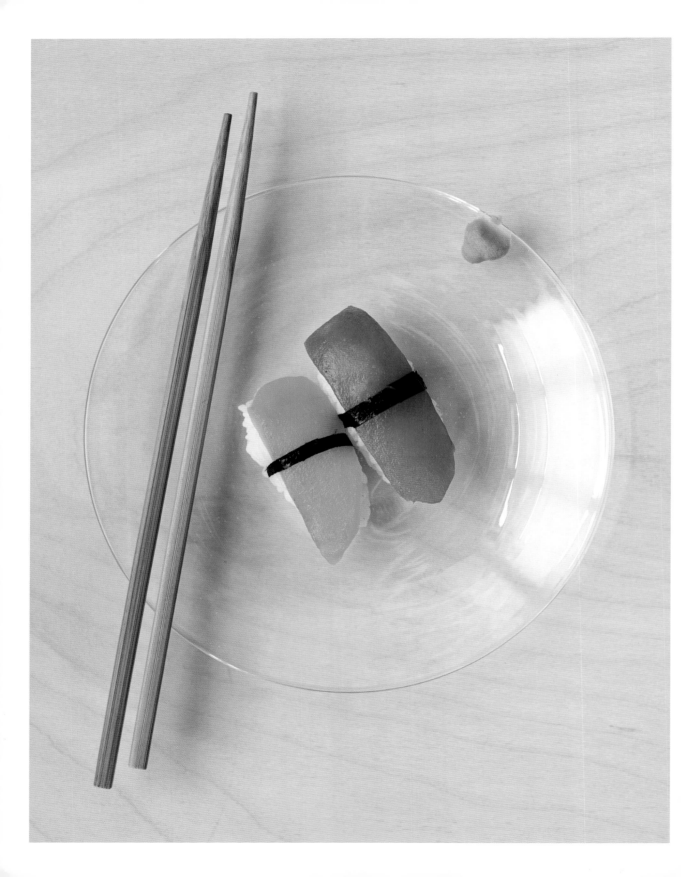

PEPPER NIGIRI SUSHI

Nigiri sushi is made by molding with your hands. For a step-by-step guide to forming it, see page 21.

Makes 12

— **2 bell peppers** (1 red, 1 yellow)
— **1⅓ cups [240 g] White sushi rice, cooked and seasoned with sushi vinegar, lukewarm** (see page 110)
— **1 full sheet of dried nori seaweed**

Grill the peppers, turning, until the skin is blackened on all sides. Leave until cool, then peel the peppers, remove the ribs, stem and seeds and cut each into 6 neat strips, 2½-by-1¼-in [6-by-3-cm].

Using ¹/₁₂ [20 g] of rice each time and following my guide (see page 21), make 12 nigiri rice shapes. Place a piece of red or yellow pepper on top of

ZEN SUSHI

I call this "Zen" because it is vegan, in the tradition of the food eaten by Japanese monks. For a step-by-step guide to how to roll sushi, see page 21.

Serves 1

— **6 asparagus spears**
— **Sea salt**
— **4 oyster mushrooms, sliced**
— **2 heaping Tbsp [20 g] white sesame seeds**
— **Heaping ¾ cup [150 g] White sushi rice, cooked and seasoned with sushi vinegar, lukewarm** (see page 110)
— **1 half sheet of nori seaweed.**

Steam the asparagus spears over salty water for 3 or 4 minutes, or until just becoming tender. Drain very well.

Preheat the broiler to its highest setting. Broil the asparagus and mushrooms, sprinkled with sea salt, on both sides, until cooked.

Mix the sesame seeds into the rice.

Place the sheet of nori on a sushi rolling mat, rough side up. Place the rice over the entire sheet of nori. Flip the sheet upside down so the seaweed is on the top, facing you. It should still be on the rolling mat.

Place the asparagus spears and mushrooms in the center of the seaweed.

Then, using the rolling mat, roll the whole length up. Cut into 6 pieces, then serve.

SUSHI CANAPÉS

These are easy to make in large batches for a party,
You will need a 1¼ in [3 cm] cookie cutter. Use the
same shape or different shapes, as you prefer.

Each recipe makes 10

— **1 heaping cup [200 g] White sushi rice,**
cooked and seasoned with sushi vinegar,
lukewarm (see page 110)

Make 10 bases by packing the cutter with
¹/₁₀ [20 g] rice. Add the toppings (see below),
before gently removing the cutter.

CRAB CANAPÉS

— **1 Tbsp mayonnaise**
— **Pinch of chopped dill, plus spriglets to serve**
— **2 Tbsp [20 g] flaked crab**
— **10 parsley leaves, finely chopped**

Mix the mayonnaise and dill together.
Spoon the mayo onto the rice canapé.

Place a small amount of flaked crab
on top and finish with a parsley leaf
and a little dill.

SALMON ROE WASABI CANAPÉS

— **1 tsp wasabi paste**
— **1¼ in [3 cm] chunk of cucumber, minced**
— **2 Tbsp salmon roe**
— **A few pea shoots**

Mix the wasabi and cucumber together.
Spoon this on to the rice canapé.

Place the salmon roe on top of this and
finish with the pea shoots.

FRUITY SALMON FLOWER CANAPÉS

— **10 small slices of melon**
— **5 oba or arugula leaves**
— **2 slices of smoked salmon, each cut into 5**

Place a slice of melon on top of the rice canapé.
Cut each oba leaf into 4 and add 2 on top of each
slice of melon (so it looks as if it is the leaf
of a flower).

Roll a smoked salmon piece up to make a flower bud
shape and place it on top.

SPICY ZUCCHINI CANAPÉS

— **Scant 3 Tbsp [20 g] white turnip, cut into**
¼ in [5 mm] cubes
— **Sea salt**
— **1¼ in [3 cm] length of zucchini, sliced into**
¼ in [5 mm] strips
— **Scant 2 Tbsp [10 g] grated cheddar cheese**
— **1 tsp grapeseed oil**
— **1 tsp wasabi paste**
— **1 tsp maple syrup**

Place the turnip in a bowl, sprinkle with sea
salt, and set aside to marinate for 20 minutes.
Drain in a sieve.

Meanwhile, preheat the broiler, or heat a griddle
pan. Lightly broil, or griddle, the zucchini slices
on both sides for a few minutes. Put a little cheese
on top of each zucchini slice and broil for two
minutes. Place each slice of zucchini on top of
a rice canapé.

Mix the marinated turnip, grapeseed oil, and wasabi.
Spoon this on top of the zucchini.

Add a tiny drop of syrup to serve.

Index

A

adzuki beans: bean salad 68
apples: brown rice tuna sushi 107
    fruit buns 65
    sweet potato treat 65
asparagus: Japanese grilled vegetable "stir-fry" 72
    zen sushi 119
avocados: avocado and pear quinoa power sushi 102
    bouquet of flowers temaki 111
    broiled avocado 75
    5 senses super-tasty salmon sushi 115
    flower cake 112
    salmon, roe and avocado sushi cake 112

B

bacon: bacon and cabbage steamed pudding 54
    Japanese garden 60
bamboo: broiled spring rolls 79
bass: see sea bass
beans 13
    see also adzuki beans, edamame beans etc
beansprouts: ginger chicken with beansprouts 50
    Japanese grilled vegetable "stir-fry" 72
beef: shabu shabu 41
Belgian endive with cod roe salad 94
bitter tastes 9
black beans 8
bouquet of flowers temaki 111
breakfast, "full Japanese" 54
British pork dumplings 53
broccoli 8
    Japanese garden 60
broiling 14, 67
broth, vegetable 40
brown rice tuna sushi with sweet-hot sauce 107
brown shiitake and pumpkin sushi 104
brown sushi rice 104
buckwheat 8
buns, fruit 65
burger, Japanese 68

C

cabbage 8
    bacon and cabbage steamed pudding 54
    posh dinner in 20 minutes 48
canapés, sushi 120
carrots 8
    Japanese grilled vegetable "stir-fry" 72
    posh dinner in 20 minutes 48
celery: Belgian endive with cod roe salad 94
cellophane noodle soup 26
cheese: spicy zucchini canapés 120
    sushi cup cakes 111
    wasabi cream cheese sushi 117
chicken: chicken lemon pot 57
    ginger chicken with beansprouts 50
    gluten-free chicken sausages 47
    hot steamed chicken 60
    Japanese soufflé 63
    mustard chicken 79
    shrimp pillow 50
    spicy steamed chicken salad 48
    steamed sticky rice 58
chickpeas: Japanese burger 68
chili tofu 77
cod: Maki's cod miso 80
    posh dinner in 20 minutes 48
cod roe: Belgian endive with cod roe salad 94
colors 7–8
cooking methods 14–15
cilantro leaves: iced tomato 92
corn 8
zucchini: full of goodness 75
    spicy zucchini canapés 120
crab canapés 120
crackers, Maki's rice 85
cream cheese sushi 117
cucumber 8
    bouquet of flowers temaki 111
    cucumber soup 36
    egg and eel sushi roll 115
    flower cake 112
    Japanese pickles 90
    sesame seed salmon sushi 110
    vinegared shrimp salad 89

D

dairy produce 13
dancing shrimp 29
dashi 9, 18
    egg and tofu dashi soup 36
    Japanese soufflé 63
    Motoko's (my mother's) dashi 18
    noodle soup stock 18
    soup stock 18
    vegetarian dashi 18
doll cakes 117
dressings 19–20
dumplings, British pork 53

E

edamame beans 8
    edamame soup 30
    shrimp pillow 50
    pumpkin of plenty! 57
    spicy edamame 30
eel: egg and eel sushi roll 115
eggplant: eggplant and shallot salad 72
    stuffed vegetables 53
eggs 13
    doll cakes 117
    egg and eel sushi roll 115
    egg and tofu dashi soup 36
    flower cake 112
    "full Japanese" garden breakfast 54
    Japanese soufflé 63
enoki mushrooms: steamed sticky rice 58
eyesight 10

F

fish 8, 13
    sushi 15, 21
      see also cod, salmon etc.
5 senses super-tasty salmon sushi 115
flower cake 112
food groups 12–13
fruit 13
fruit buns 65
fruity salmon flower canapés 120
frying 14, 67
full of goodness 75
"full Japanese" garden breakfast 54

G

garden soy sauce dressing 20
ginger: ginger chicken with beansprouts 50
    ginger sardines 40
gluten-free chicken sausages 47
glutinous rice: Maki's rice crackers 85
    steamed sticky rice 58
grains 12
green beans: bean salad 68
grilling 14, 67

H

heavenly steamed sea bream 47
honey: honey tomato with tofu 94
    sweet potato treat 65

I

iced tomato 92
inside-out sushi rolls 21

J

Japanese burger 68
Japanese cellophane noodle soup 26
Japanese garden 60
Japanese grilled vegetable "stir-fry" 72
Japanese pickles 90
Japanese soufflé 63
julienning vegetables 15

K

kale: "full Japanese" garden breakfast 54
    kale salad 98

L

lamb: wasabi cream cheese sushi 117
leeks: chili tofu 77
    shabu shabu 41
lemon: chicken lemon pot 57
    lemon soy sauce dressing 20
lettuce: shabu shabu 41
    spinach salad 92
lotus root: full of goodness 75

M

mackerel: Japanese cellophane noodle soup 26
Maki's cod miso 80
Maki's miso pork 82
Maki's rice crackers 85
mangoes: avocado and pear quinoa power sushi 102
maple syrup: spicy zucchini canapés 120
meat 13
melon: fruity salmon flower canapés 120
microwave ovens 14, 45
miso: Maki's cod miso 80
    Maki's miso pork 82
mochi, sweet soy sauce 63
daikon 8
    chicken lemon pot 57
    Japanese garden 60
    Maki's cod miso 80
    daikon steak 58
Motoko's (my mother's) dashi 18
mushrooms 8
    broiled spring rolls 79
    brown shiitake and pumpkin sushi 104
    dancing shrimp 29
    egg and eel sushi roll 115
    "full Japanese" garden breakfast 54
    Japanese soufflé 63
    rice noodles with mushroom broth 26
    steamed sticky rice 58
    zen sushi 119
mustard chicken 79

N

Napa cabbage 8
    chicken lemon pot 57
    Japanese pickles 90
nigiri 21
    pepper nigiri sushi 119
noodle soup stock 18
noodles: Japanese cellophane noodle soup 26
    rice noodles with mushroom broth 26
    soba soup 33
nori seaweed: avocado and pear quinoa power sushi 102
    bouquet of flowers temaki 111
    brown rice tuna sushi with sweet-hot sauce 107
    brown shiitake and pumpkin sushi 104
    doll cakes 117
    egg and eel sushi roll 115
    5 senses super-tasty salmon sushi 115
    pepper nigiri sushi 119
    sesame seed salmon sushi 110
    spinach salad 92
    wasabi cream cheese sushi 117
    zen sushi 119
nuts 13

O

oba leaves: bouquet of flowers temaki 111
    iced tomato 92
okra: grilled avocado 75

okra with canned tuna **98**
onions: Japanese pickles **90**
oranges: fruit buns **65**
    Maki's miso pork **82**
oyster mushrooms: dancing shrimp **29**
    zen sushi **119**

P

pan tai **34**
pears: avocado and pear quinoa power sushi **102**
peppers: full of goodness **75**
    pepper nigiri sushi **119**
    stuffed vegetables **53**
perfect with beer dressing **20**
pickles, Japanese **90**
pork: British pork dumplings **53**
    broiled spring rolls **79**
    Maki's miso pork **82**
    soba soup **33**
posh dinner in 20 minutes **48**
prosciutto: sushi cup cakes **111**
pumpkin **8**
    brown shiitake and pumpkin sushi **104**
    full of goodness **75**
    Japanese garden **60**
    pumpkin of plenty! **57**

Q

quail eggs: doll cakes **117**
quinoa: avocado and pear quinoa power sushi **102**

R

raw food **14–15, 87**
rice **8**
    bouquet of flowers temaki **111**
    brown rice tuna sushi with sweet-hot sauce **107**
    brown sushi rice **104**
    doll cakes **117**
    egg and eel sushi roll **115**
    5 senses super-tasty salmon sushi **115**
    flower cake **112**
    Maki's rice crackers **85**
    pan tai **34**
    pepper nigiri sushi **119**
    salmon, roe and avocado sushi cake **112**
    sesame seed salmon sushi **110**
    steamed sticky rice **58**
    sushi **15, 21**
    sushi canapés **120**
    sushi cup cakes **111**
    wasabi cream cheese sushi **117**
    white sushi rice **110**
    zen sushi **119**
rice flour: sweet soy sauce mochi **63**
rice noodles with mushroom broth **26**
rice paper: shrimp pillow **50**
roe: Belgian endive with cod roe salad **94**
    flower cake **112**
    salmon, roe and avocado sushi cake **112**
    salmon roe wasabi canapés **120**
rosemary soy sauce dressing **19**

S

sake: sweet potato treat **65**
salads: eggplant and shallot salad **72**
    bean salad **68**
    Belgian endive with cod roe salad **94**
    honey tomato with tofu **94**
    kale salad **98**
    spicy steamed chicken salad **48**
    spinach salad **92**
    vinegared shrimp salad **89**
salmon: bouquet of flowers temaki **111**
    five senses super-tasty salmon sushi **115**
    flower cake **112**
    salmon, roe and avocado sushi cake **112**
    sesame seed salmon sushi **110**
    sushi cup cakes **111**
salmon roe: flower cake **112**
    salmon, roe and avocado sushi cake **112**
    salmon roe wasabi canapés **120**
salt **9**
sardines, ginger **40**
sausages, gluten-free chicken **47**
scallops: posh dinner in 20 minutes **48**
sea bass: bouquet of flowers temaki **111**
    heavenly steamed sea bream **47**
    pan tai **34**
    soba soup **33**
    sushi cup cakes **111**
seaweed **8**
    avocado and pear quinoa power sushi **102**
    bouquet of flowers temaki **111**
    brown rice tuna sushi with sweet-hot sauce **107**
    brown shiitake and pumpkin sushi **104**
    doll cakes **117**
    egg and eel sushi roll **115**
    five senses super-tasty salmon sushi **115**
    pepper nigiri sushi **119**
    sesame seed salmon sushi **110**
    spinach salad **92**
    vinegared shrimp salad **89**
    wasabi cream cheese sushi **117**
    zen sushi **119**
seeds **13**
    see also sesame seeds
senses **10**
sesame seeds **8**
    flower cake **112**
    kale salad **98**
    sesame salad sprinkle dressing **19**
    sesame seed salmon sushi **110**
    spinach salad **92**
    sushi cup cakes **111**
    wasabi cream cheese sushi **117**
    zen sushi **119**
shabu shabu **41**
shabu shabu dressing **20**
shallots: eggplant and shallot salad **72**
shiitake mushrooms **8**
    broiled spring rolls **79**
    brown shiitake and pumpkin sushi **104**
    egg and eel sushi roll **115**
    "full Japanese" garden breakfast **54**
    Japanese soufflé **63**

rice noodles with mushroom broth **26**
shrimp: bouquet of flowers temaki **111**
    dancing shrimp **29**
    Japanese soufflé **63**
    shrimp barbecue **70**
    shrimp pillow **50**
    vinegared shrimp salad **89**
sight **10**
simmering **14, 25**
smell, sense of **10**
smoked cod roe: Belgian endive with cod roe salad **94**
smoked mackerel: Japanese cellophane noodle soup **26**
smoked salmon: bouquet of flowers temaki **111**
    fruity salmon flower canapés **120**
    salmon, roe and avocado sushi cake **112**
    sushi cup cakes **111**
snow peas: Japanese garden **60**
soba soup **33**
soufflé, Japanese **63**
sounds **10**
soups: cucumber soup **36**
    edamame soup **30**
    egg and tofu dashi soup **36**
    Japanese cellophane noodle soup **26**
    soba soup **33**
    stocks **18**
    vegetable broth **40**
sour tastes **9**
soybeans **8**
    stuffed vegetables **53**
soy sauce: dressings **19–20**
    Maki's rice crackers **85**
    sweet soy sauce mochi **63**
spinach **8**
    egg and eel sushi roll **115**
    egg and tofu dashi soup **36**
    "full Japanese" garden breakfast **54**
    Japanese grilled vegetable "stir-fry" **72**
    spinach salad **92**
scallions: shrimp barbecue **70**
spring rolls, broiled **79**
steamed pudding, bacon and cabbage **54**
steaming **14, 45**
sticky rice, steamed **58**
stocks **18**
sushi **15, 21, 101**
    avocado and pear quinoa power sushi **102**
    bouquet of flowers temaki **111**
    brown rice tuna sushi with sweet-hot sauce **107**
    brown shiitake and pumpkin sushi **104**
    brown sushi rice **104**
    doll cakes **117**
    egg and eel sushi roll **115**
    five senses super-tasty salmon sushi **115**
    flower cake **112**
    pepper nigiri sushi **119**
    salmon, roe and avocado sushi cake **112**
    sesame seed salmon sushi **110**
    sushi canapés **120**
    sushi cup cakes **111**
    sushi rolls **21**
    wasabi cream cheese sushi **117**
    white sushi rice **110**
    zen sushi **119**
sweet potatoes **8**
    sweet potato dream **85**

sweet potato treat **65**
sweet soy dressing **19**
sweet soy sauce mochi **63**
sweet tastes **9**

T

taste, sense of **10**
tastes, five **9**
temaki, bouquet of flowers **111**
tiger shrimp: shrimp barbecue **70**
tofu: chili tofu **77**
    egg and tofu dashi soup **36**
    honey tomato with tofu **94**
    Japanese burger **68**
    pumpkin of plenty! **57**
    soba soup **33**
tomatoes **8**
    full of goodness **75**
    "full Japanese" garden breakfast **54**
    broiled avocado **75**
    honey tomato with tofu **94**
    iced tomato **92**
    stuffed vegetables **53**
touch, sense of **10**
tuna: bouquet of flowers temaki **111**
    brown rice tuna sushi with sweet-hot sauce **107**
    flower cake **112**
    okra with canned tuna **98**
    sushi cup cakes **111**
turkey: Japanese burger **68**
    shrimp pillow **50**
turnips: Japanese garden **60**
    Japanese pickles **90**
    spicy zucchini canapés **120**

U

umami **9**

V

vegetables **13**
    full of goodness **75**
    Japanese garden **60**
    Japanese grilled vegetable "stir-fry" **72**
    julienning **15**
    stuffed vegetables **53**
    vegetable broth **40**
    see also avocados, tomatoes etc.
vegetarian dashi **18**
vinegared shrimp salad **89**

W

wasabi: salmon roe wasabi canapés **120**
    spicy zucchini canapés **120**
    wasabi cream cheese sushi **117**
white sushi rice **110**
wonton sheets: British pork dumplings **53**

Z

zen sushi **119**

Thanks once again to everyone at Quadrille, especially to Anne Furniss for her continued faith in me and to Helen Lewis for her amazing eye and for finding just the right team to make this such a beautiful book. Lisa Linder, that means you! And to Risa Sano and Aya Nishimura for the design and for making all the food look so incredible.

To Diana Beaumont, for your efficiency, warmth and spot-on judgement. Thank you. To Emma Bannister, for all your experience, patience, hard work and lots of laughs. Thanks to Lucy Bannell, for your work and support.

Most especially, to my mother and my grandmother, Motoko and Teru.

Editorial director Anne Furniss
Creative director Helen Lewis
Project editor Lucy Bannell
Art direction and design Mentsen
Photography Lisa Linder
Editorial consultant Emma Bannister
Food styling Aya Nishimura
Production director Vincent Smith
Production controller Emily Noto

First published in 2015 by Quadrille Publishing
www.quadrille.co.uk

Quadrille is an imprint of Hardie Grant
www.hardiegrant.com.au

Text © 2015 Makiko Sano
Photography © 2015 Lisa Linder
Design & layout © 2015 Quadrille Publishing Ltd

British Library Cataloguing-in-Publication Data
A catalogue record for this book is available from the British Library.

ISBN: 978 184949 669 8

Printed in China.